SURE & SIMPLE

DO·IT·YOURSELF

This edition published 1976 by
Mills and Boon Limited,
17–19 Foley Street, London W1A 1DR

ISBN 0 263 06011 X

Filmset by Ramsay Typesetters
(Crawley) Ltd, through Reynolds Clark
Associates Ltd, London
Printed in Italy by New Interlitho S.P.A.

Sure and Simple Series
created and produced by
Sackett Publishing Services Ltd,
104 Great Portland Street, London W1N 5PE

SURE & SIMPLE DO-IT-YOURSELF

Harry Butler

Illustrated by Tri-Art

Designed by
Keith Groom and Cyril Mason

Mills & Boon Limited

London

CONTENTS

Know your Tools

An essential part of any D.I.Y. job is to use the correct tool, properly sharpened and adjusted and with the correct technique for the work in hand. For this reason the major part of this book is concerned with just this type of vital information. The basic types of tools are fully illustrated and the various techniques of use and application illustrated and explained.

The range of tools covered is wide but it is not of course suggested that the home handyman should possess them all. Indeed an important function of the book is that it can be used as a catalogue to assist in tool selection, thus avoiding the often wasteful and costly process of buying and using tools by trial and error.

Once the application of simple tools is understood, then progress can be made toward putting them to useful work. Whatever project is to be tackled, from making a simple shelf to complete house decoration, the end result will benefit much from a good knowledge and understanding of the use and limitations of the tools involved.

Drills and Drilling

Basic drilling tools are shown opposite and consist of:

A *Carpenter's Brace.* Several varieties of this tool are available from the small electrician's type (top) to the standard ratchet type (bottom). The chuck jaws may be either of the alligator type, for gripping square shanked auger bits (E overleaf) or of the universal type which will also hold round shanked bits. Generally used for carpentry work in conjunction with the auger bit.

B *Hand Drills.* These may be either single or double pinion and with open or enclosed gears, and are intended for comparatively light work in wood, metal, plastic or masonry.

C *Engineer's Drills (Breast).* Again these may be of the open or enclosed gear type and often incorporate a two speed gearing arrangement. Intended for heavier work in metal or masonry, but can be used for wood or plastic.

D *Electric Drill.* Single speed drills, normally rated at 2,900 r.p.m. generally have a chuck with a capacity of about 6 mm ($\frac{1}{4}$″) and may be used for drilling wood, metal, plastic or masonry. Care must be taken when drilling hard metal or masonry, or large holes in wood, not to overload the tool by excessive pressure. It is important the motor runs smoothly and at a fast speed. With two-speed geared drills, the slow speed should be used for heavy work. Because the gearing extends the range of usage, a larger chuck, up to about 15 mm ($\frac{1}{2}$″) is often fitted.

E *Drill Stand.* The drill stand is a useful accessory for the power drill.

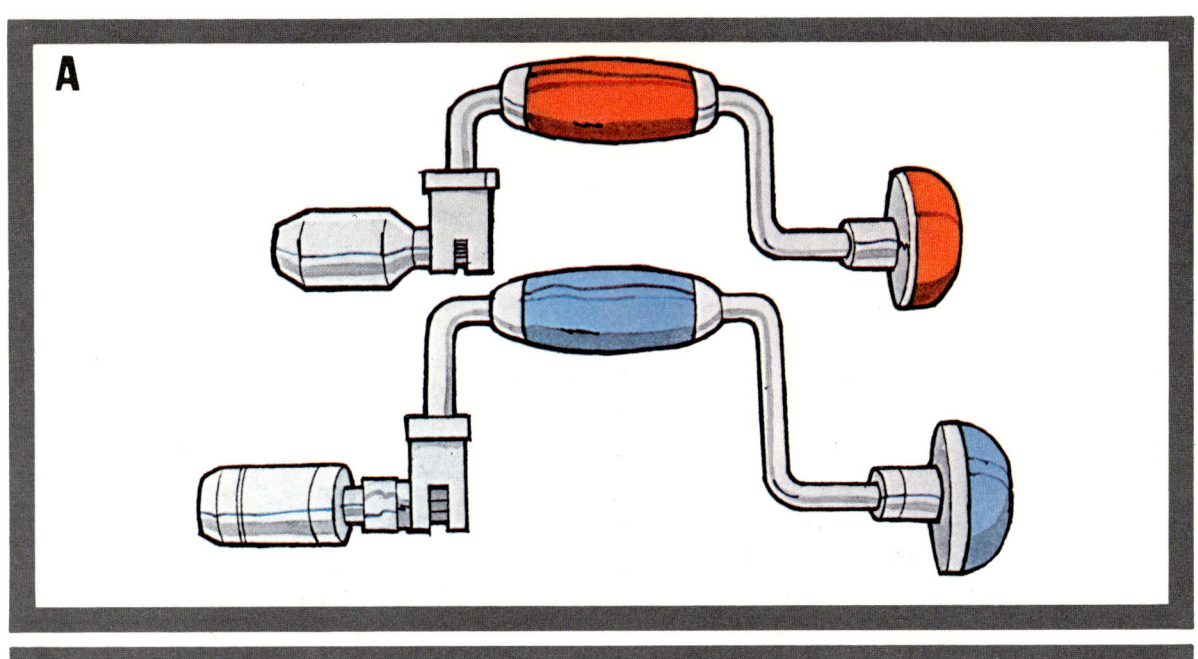

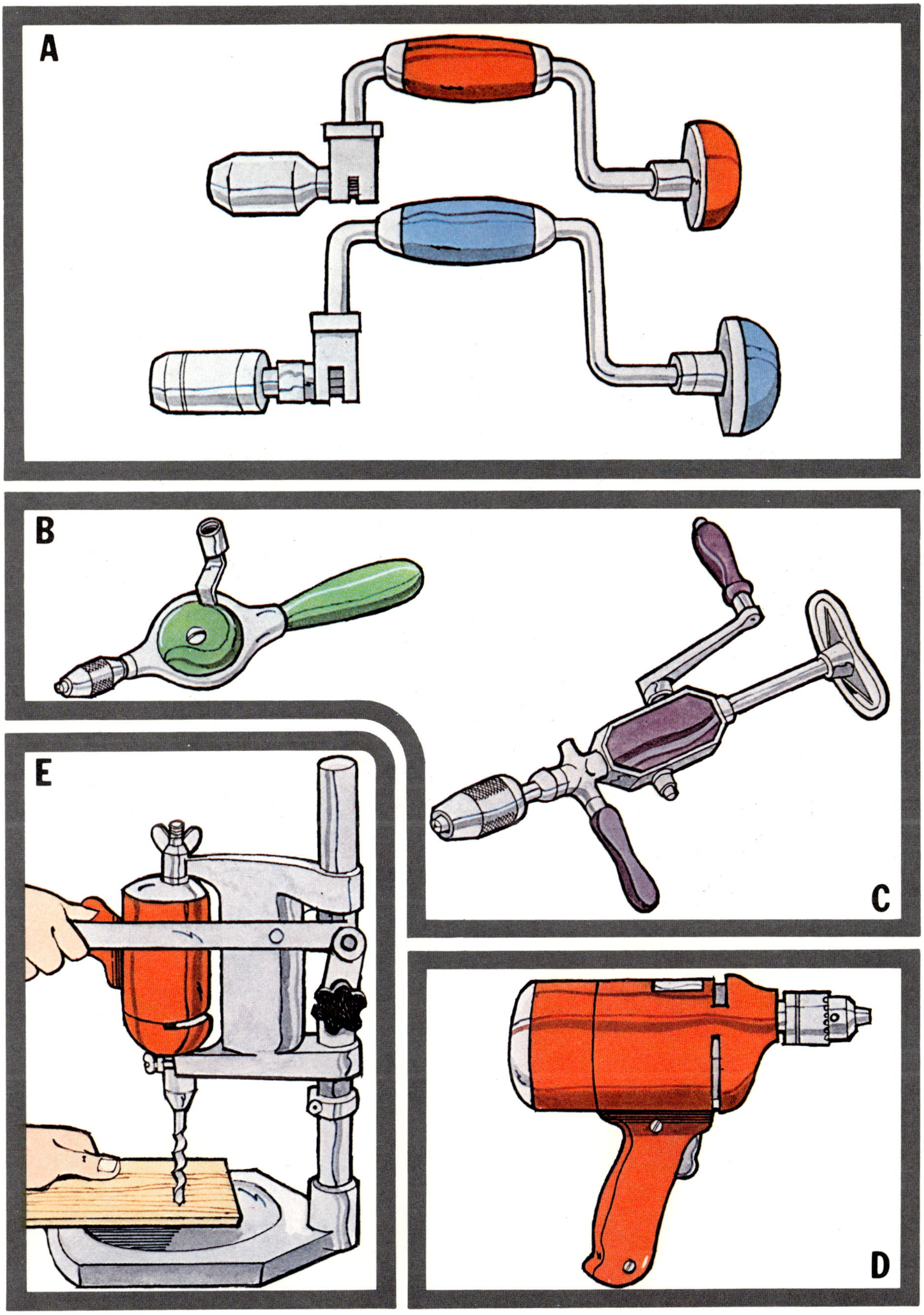

A

B

E

C

D

Drilling Techniques

Metal

A centre punch should be used to mark the hole location and also to provide a start for the drill, *see Fig. 2*. Thin sheet metal should be clamped to a piece of timber to provide a clean drill exit hole. With thick metal care must be taken not to overheat the bit, thereby softening the metal through loss of 'temper'.

Plastic

A centre punch or bradawl should be used to mark the hole centre and to provide a start for the drill. The drill speed should be kept low and pressure light, as the plastic may crack, distort or melt if overheated. Sheet material should be firmly clamped to a timber backing to provide a clean drill exit hole.

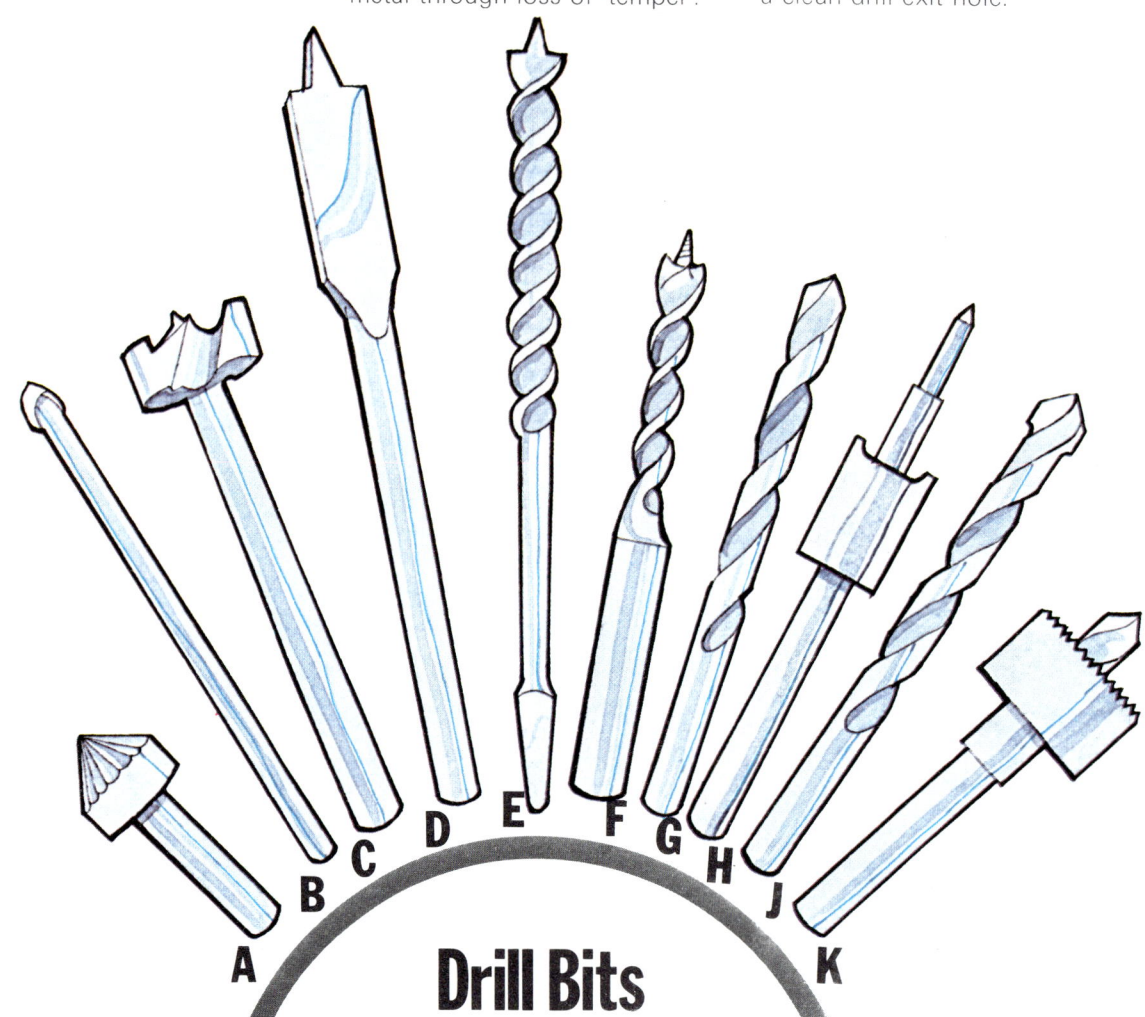

Drill Bits

	Type	Use	Remarks
A	Countersink bit	Wood, metal, plastic	Hand and Power
B	Spear point bit	Glass, ceramic tiles	Hand and Power
C	Forstner bit	Wood	Power
D	Flat-bit	Wood – some plastics	Power
E	Auger	Wood	Hand
F	Dowel bit	Wood	Power
G	Twist drill	Metal, plastic, wood	Hand and Power
H	Combination screw bit	Wood, plastic	Hand and Power
J	Masonry bit	Masonry, ceramic tiles	Hand and Power
K	Hole Saw	Wood, metal, plastic	Hand and Power

Glass

For holes up to about $\frac{5}{16}$" (8 mm) the drill speed must be no more than about 900 r.p.m. Light pressure should be applied and the drill lubricated with turpentine or paraffin. A small reservoir built up from putty around the hole may be used to contain the liquid, *Fig. 1*. After the bit has pierced through, the work should be turned over and drilling continued from the reverse side. Never use the drill dry.

Masonry

Always use a slow speed as masonry drills are easily overheated through friction. Where the surface is extra hard, constantly break contact between bit and masonry and keep the spirals and hole clear of dust.

Wood

Generally with power tools a fast speed will produce the cleanest cut, but with large holes or extra hard wood a slow gearing should be selected (where fitted) to avoid overloading the drill motor. When drilling 'through' holes with a power tool, a piece of timber should be firmly cramped to the underside of the work to provide a clean drill exit hole, *Fig. 3*. With the hand auger bit, work should be finished from the reverse side immediately the threaded tip breaks through. The combination screw bit is designed to cut 3 sizes of hole in one operation. The tip cuts a pilot hole for the screw threads, the centre part a shank clearance hole and the angle shaped top part, a countersink. When using the screw combination bit the two pieces of wood to be joined should be either nailed or clamped together during the drilling operation (**H**).

Most types of holesaw consist of a conventional central twist drill bit fitted with a machined cup to which circular, interchangeable hole cutting blades, of varying sizes, are fitted (**K**).

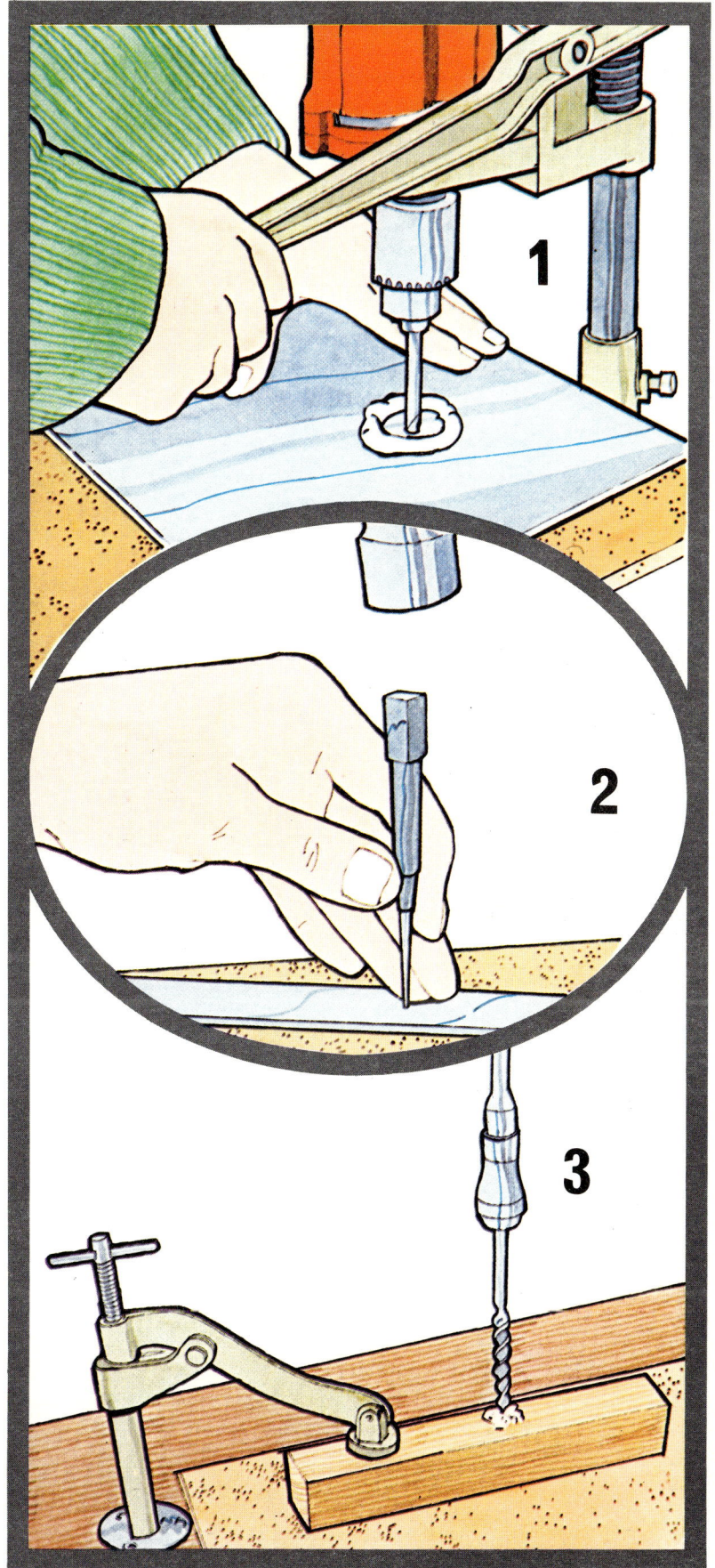

Measuring and Marking

Accurate marking and measuring is the basis of any well executed project, and care taken at this stage will always be well rewarded in the final job. Even a simple task (cutting a piece of timber to length, for instance) demands careful marking if a clean and accurate cut is to be achieved.

A A carpenter's pencil with a rectangular lead which, when sharpened 'chisel style' as illustrated, will produce a more consistent and therefore accurate line than the conventional round lead pencil.

B A flexible steel measuring tape, preferably fitted with a lockable blade, is a most useful feature when working single-handed. It is suitable for most general measuring jobs and can be conveniently carried in a pocket. Note that with most rules of this type 'inside' measurements can be taken provided the

H

B

15   16

C

9   10   11

230   24(0)   250   2(0)   270   280   290   3(0)

working. The square is used for initial marking (*see Fig. 1*) before cutting; for checking the accuracy of timber sections, cut ends and joints; and during assembly or construction to ensure accurate mating and alignment of components.

E A versatile steel sliding combination square for marking 45° and 90° angles (*Fig. 2*). Can also be used as a depth gauge, or marking gauge, inside or outside try-square. Many makes also include a built-in levelling bubble.

F A sliding bevel, easily adjusted and locked to any angle and useful for marking or transferring angles accurately.

G Engineers' or plumbers' folding steel rule. A hardwearing rule suitable for use in metal or plumbing work.

H A small spirit level used for trying and adjusting horizontals and verticals as in the case of the shelf, *see Fig. 3*. Here the left hand is used to adjust the shelf against the spirit level reading whilst screw positions are marked with a pencil held in the other hand. Note that *Fig. 3* illustrates two methods of shelf bracket fixing, i.e. supported from below (the white bracket) or suspended from above (the black bracket). In either case the spirit level would be employed in a similar manner.

width of the casing, normally marked on the side, is added to the readable measurement. A further important point to note is that the steel hook fitted to the end of the tape has elongated fixing slots allowing movement corresponding to the thickness of the metal, for accurate internal and external measurement.

C A steel 'straight edge' rule useful for setting out and scribing straight lines.

D A carpenter's try-square, essential for accurate wood-

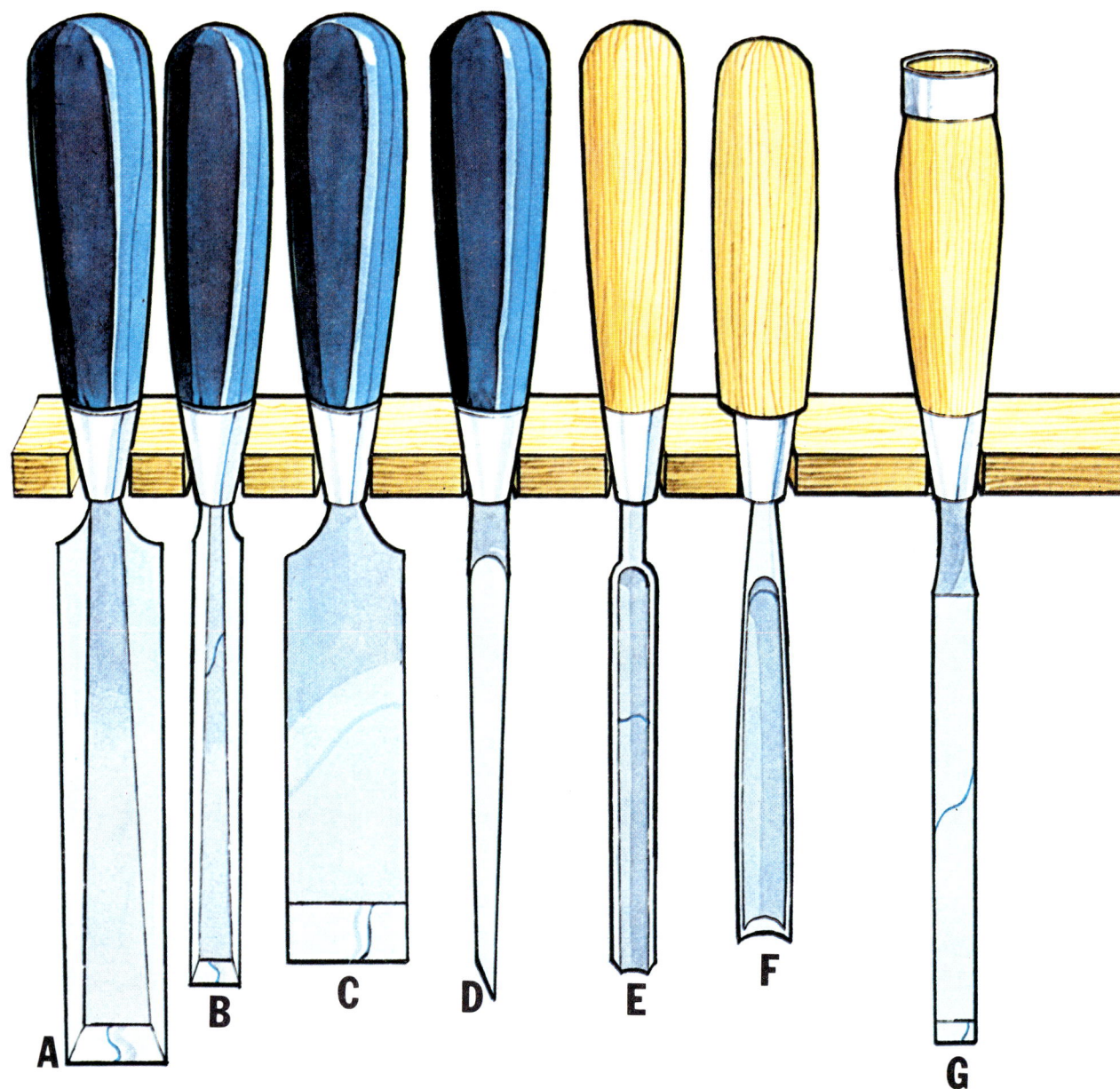

A B C D E F G

Chisels & Cutting Tools

A chisel will only perform satisfactorily if the cutting edge is really sharp. A blunt or damaged edge not only ruins the work but, more important, can present a danger to the user, because of the undue pressure required when attempting to force a cut.

An essential accessory for storing chisels in the workshop is a rack similar to that illustrated. Laying unprotected chisels on the bench or in a toolbox often results in cutting edge damage and again presents a potential hazard to hands searching for tools. Where chisels must be put in a box or on the shelf, then purpose-made plastic edge-protectors should be fitted.

Chisels are intended for cutting wood and should be used for no other purpose — it is for this reason that a multi-purpose knife has been included in the suggested chisel kit. This, together with an assortment of blades, will then always be to hand for use on material other than wood, thus removing the

temptation to use a chisel.

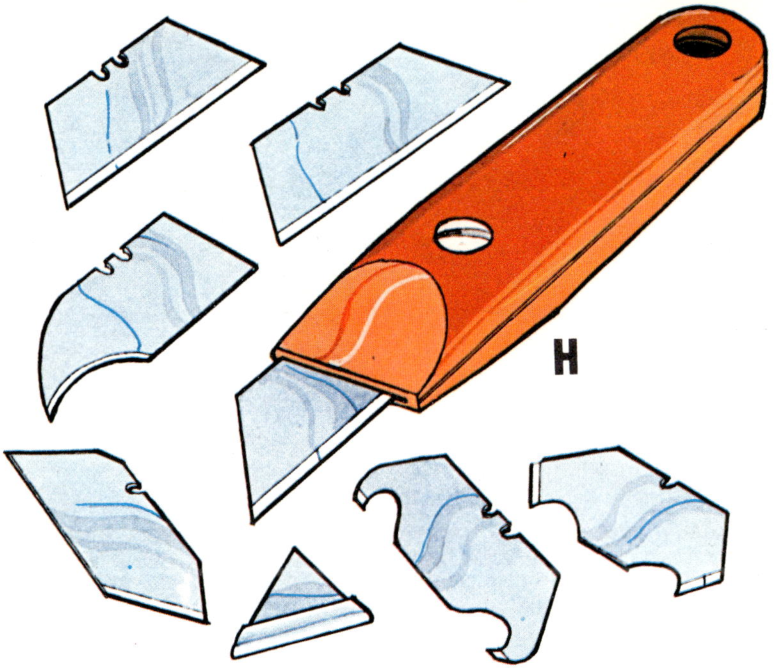

When using a chisel, or indeed any cutting tool, certain safety rules apply. Firstly and most important, the hands must always remain behind the cutting edge. The chisel must at all times remain under control, and all 'loose' work must be firmly cramped to leave both hands free. *Figs. 1, 2 and 3* illustrate this point; where the left hand is used as a 'steady' between chisel blade and work, whilst thumb pressure, applied to the face of the blade, is used to control the location of the cutting edge, pressure to the cutting edge is applied by the right hand. Where the chisel is used for paring, *Figs. 1 and 3*, a flat piece of softwood should be placed under the cut to prevent damage to the workbench, and produce a clean exit edge to the cut. It also presents a surface which will not unduly dull the chisel cutting edge.

The gouge is controlled in a similar manner when used for cutting a groove, *Fig. 2*. Here the palm of the right hand can be used to gently 'tap' the chisel into the work. Chisels illustrated are as follows:

A and **B** Bevel type, i.e. rectangular section and blade with bevelled edges, suitable for working in confined cuts.

C Firmer type i.e. plain rectangular blade suitable for general purpose work.

D Side view of a mortise chisel showing the strengthened blade intended to withstand the extra strain of mallet cutting a mortise, *see Fig. 4*.

E Firmer gouge — held as *Fig. 1* for cutting external rounds and grooving, *see Fig. 2*.

F Scribing gouge, for cutting internal rounds, *see Fig. 1*.

G A mortise chisel with reinforced handle.

H A multi purpose knife with various interchangeable blades.

Saws and Sawing

B

C

D

E

F

G

H

1

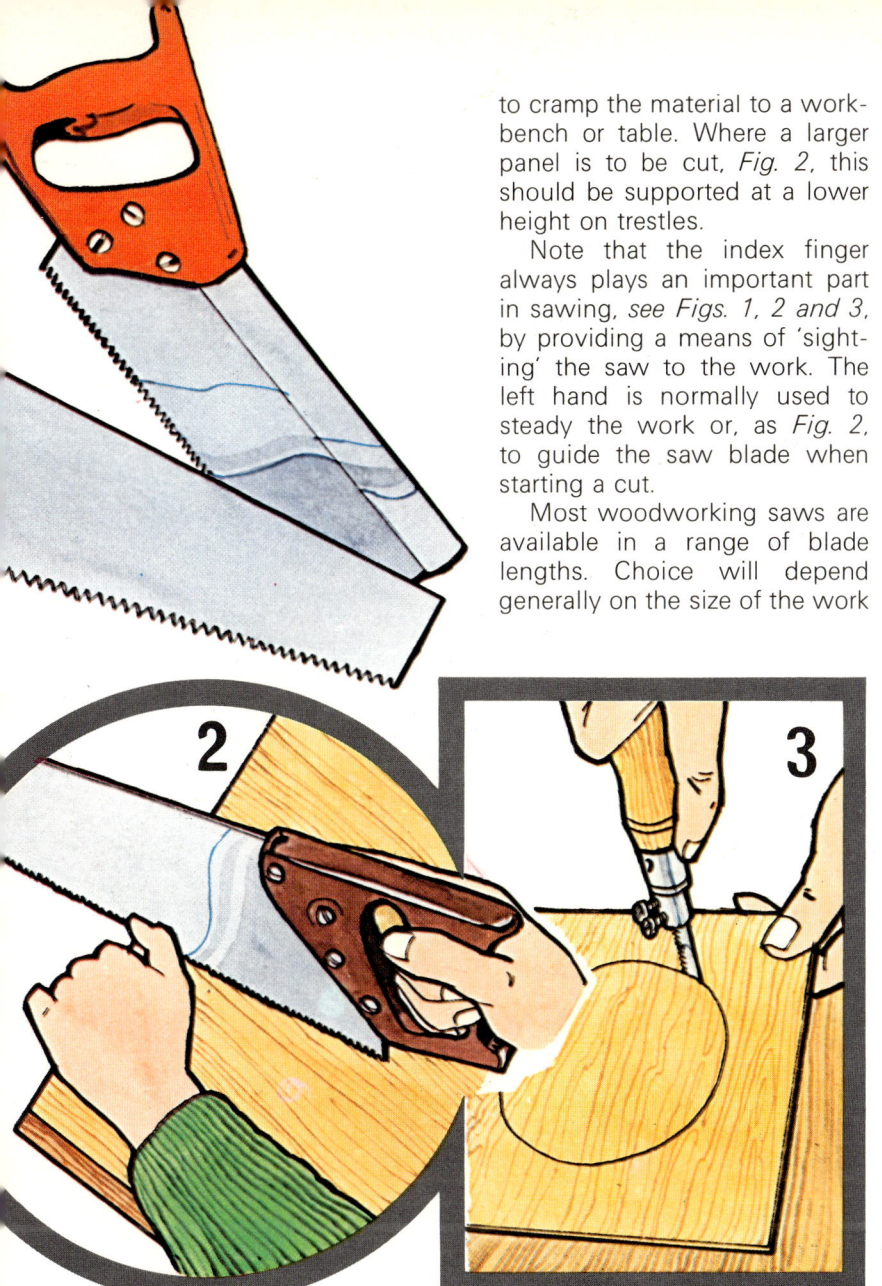

2

3

to cramp the material to a workbench or table. Where a larger panel is to be cut, *Fig. 2*, this should be supported at a lower height on trestles.

Note that the index finger always plays an important part in sawing, *see Figs. 1, 2 and 3*, by providing a means of 'sighting' the saw to the work. The left hand is normally used to steady the work or, as *Fig. 2*, to guide the saw blade when starting a cut.

Most woodworking saws are available in a range of blade lengths. Choice will depend generally on the size of the work

The ability to saw accurately is a basic technique which must be mastered before any serious woodworking project is tackled.

Saws are available in a wide range of shapes and types and the first essential is to choose one suitable for the work in hand. The material being sawn must be properly supported on a rigid platform at a comfortable working height and must be firmly held. Small pieces of wood can be conveniently held against a bench stop as *Fig. 1* or, where a curved shape is to be cut, as *Fig. 3*, it will be more convenient

to be tackled, and to some extent on the weight and build of the user. A middle-of-the-range size is suitable for most home applications.

The number of points or teeth per inch (p.p.i.) also varies. Generally a fine saw (highest p.p.i.) would be used for fine work or when working with hardwood, whilst a more coarse saw (less p.p.i.) would be used for general carpentry with softwood. Again a middle-of-the-range choice should prove suitable for most home projects.

Most woodworking saws re-

quire re-sharpening and resetting from time to time, work which is best carried out by a specialist.

A The tenon saw, used for cross-cutting strip timber, *see Fig. 1*, and also for cutting joints and grooves. Normally used on a workbench and in conjunction with a bench stop as illustrated.

B The hand or panel saw is a general purpose woodworking saw used mainly for larger carpentry work and for cutting large panels of plywood, chipboard etc., *Fig. 2*.

C A hack saw for general metal cutting. With most types the blade may be fitted to cut at several angles. Blades cannot be re-sharpened and must be replaced when worn. This type of saw is also useful for cutting plastic pipe or guttering.

D A general purpose saw with a hardened replaceable blade. The handle can be adjusted to ease working in a cramped space and the saw will cut most materials, including metal, asbestos, plastic, and wood. The inclusion of a saw of this type in the home tool kit avoids the temptation to use, and possibly ruin, a woodworking saw on an unsuitable material.

E A standard knife handle, which can be fitted with a saw blade for cutting wood (as illustrated) or metal, plastic, etc.

F A fretwork saw, available with a range of replaceable blades for fine and intricate cutting work in wood, metal, plastic, etc.

G A keyhole saw with fine pointed blade. Used mainly for cutting internal shapes, *Fig. 3*. In use a hole is first drilled, the blade inserted and then the desired shape cut.

H A coping saw, again using interchangeable blades, sprung between two anchorage points. Used for cutting internal and external curves and shapes.

Hammers
& Techniques

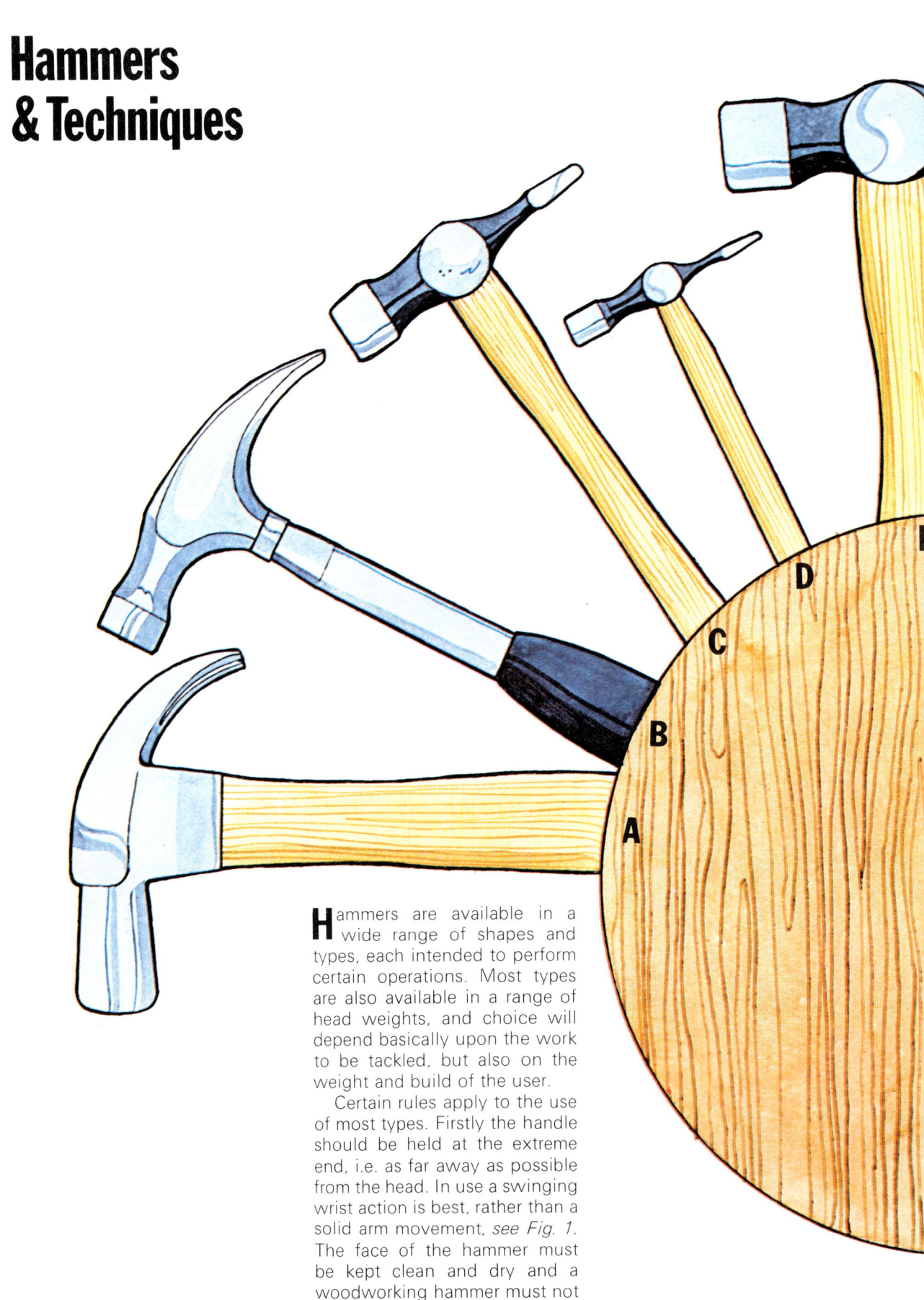

Hammers are available in a wide range of shapes and types, each intended to perform certain operations. Most types are also available in a range of head weights, and choice will depend basically upon the work to be tackled, but also on the weight and build of the user.

Certain rules apply to the use of most types. Firstly the handle should be held at the extreme end, i.e. as far away as possible from the head. In use a swinging wrist action is best, rather than a solid arm movement, *see Fig. 1.* The face of the hammer must be kept clean and dry and a woodworking hammer must not be used on hard metal or masonry surfaces, as these will bruise the face, leading to surface damage when the hammer is subsequently used on wood.

A Carpenters' claw type for general use in carpentry and larger woodworking projects. The claw is intended for removal of nails, *Fig. 2.*

B Carpenters' ripping claw. Note the shallow angle of the claw — intended as an aid to ripping up floorboards and similar work.

C Cross pien type. A general purpose hammer with a chisel shaped head useful for awkward nailing and similar work, *Fig. 3.*

D Pin hammer—available with a ball or chisel head and intended for light nailing work in carpentry and cabinet making.

E Engineers' ball type. The face of this type of hammer is harder than woodworking hammers and is intended as a general purpose engineering tool. Suitable for use with hardened nails i.e. masonry pins. The ball is useful for shaping light metal, *see Fig. 4.*

F Inter-changeable head type with screw-in facings in metal and plastic. Can be used for most hammering jobs simply by fitting the appropriate head face.

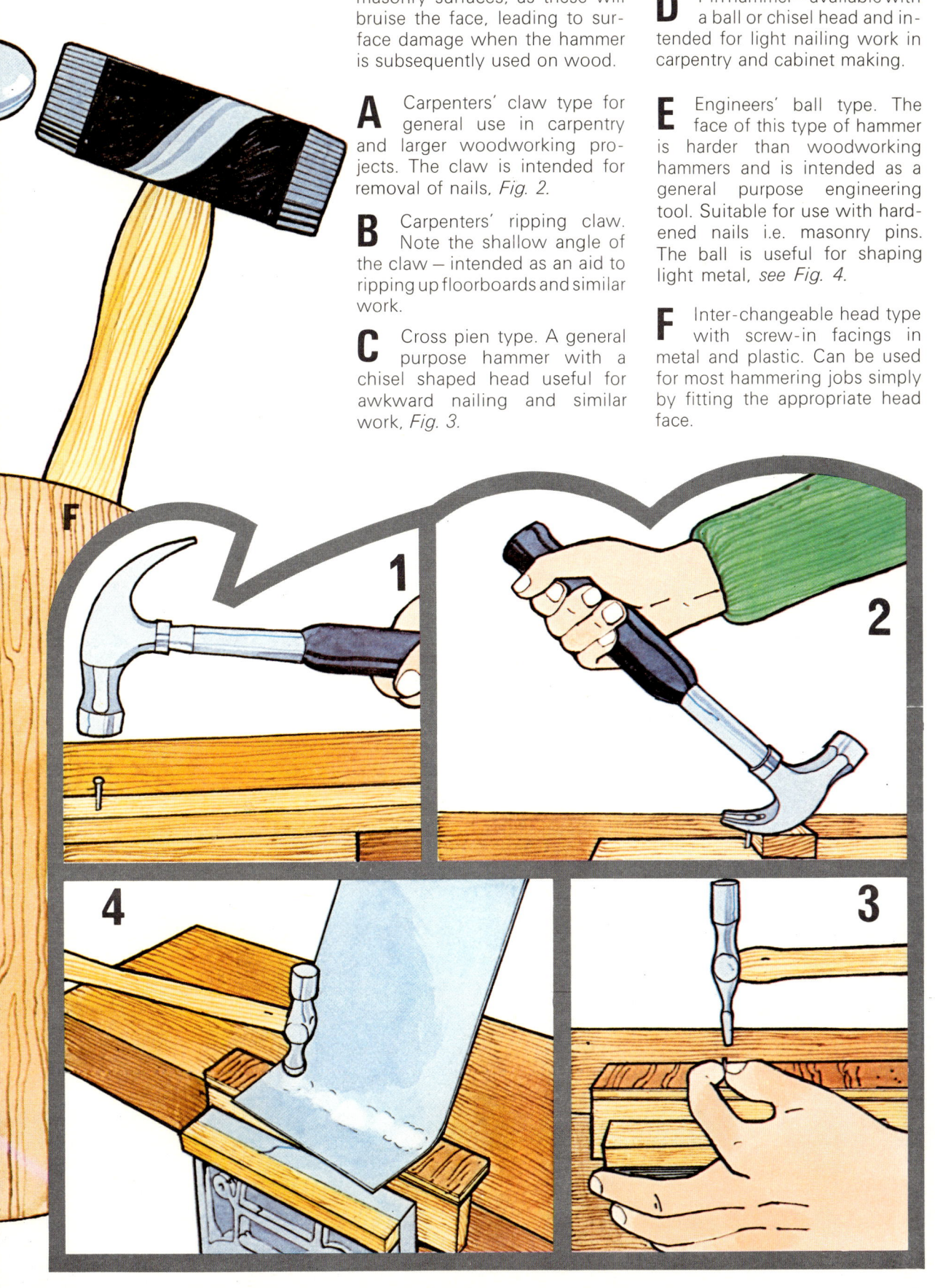

Planes and Planing

A

D

E

F

G

H

2

3

timbers. Especially useful where a true edge-to-edge joint is to be made between two boards or panels.

B A block plane in which the blade is fitted at a shallow angle for fine cutting. Ideal for planing end grain, as *Fig. 1.*

Fig. 1 illustrates a block plane 'B' being used to plane end grain. This is a particularly delicate operation in which an extra fine cut must be used. It is also important to hold the plane at a slight angle – as shown – and to plane in from either end, toward the centre. Planing straight across the end will often result in the far edge splitting away as the plane rides over.

C An ideal home handyman general purpose plane, designed to take easily replaceable throw-away blades. This type of plane is supplied complete with an adjustable guide fence for rebate cutting, *see Fig. 2.*

D A duplex rebate plane with central and forward blade positions and also fitted with an adjustable depth gauge. A somewhat specialised tool, but essential where a large number of rebates have to be accurately hand cut.

E A spokeshave for planing round and shaped edges, as *Fig. 3.*

F A rasp type plane suitable for use on wood, plastic and metal. Available in a range of sizes and shapes. The blades cannot be resharpened and must be replaced when worn.

G A combination plane designed to take a complete range of interchangeable blades used for cutting various grooves, tongues and mouldings.

H Illustrates some of the range of interchangeable blades which can be used with the combination plane **G.**

A plane will only work smoothly and produce a good job when the iron (or blade) is sharp and correctly set. Instructions for grinding and honing are covered on pages 22 and 23.

To set the blade cutting depth the plane should be held upside down and sighted along the base. The blade can then be adjusted, by means of the built-in controls, until it is square with and just visible above the base. Slight further working adjustments may be necessary depending on the type of wood being planed. Hard woods generally require a fine setting, whilst straight grained softwoods respond better to a slightly deeper cut.

An important point to check before starting the cut is the 'run' of grain in the wood. Normally when the wood is viewed from the side, the run will be biased upward in one direction. For best results the plane must always move with the uphill running grain.

A A Jack or Jointer plane available in body lengths from about 350 mm (14″) to about 550 mm (22″) and used to obtain a true edge to long

19

Cramps and Cramping

Cramps and vices play an important part in many projects, by providing a useful 'third hand'. They can also be used to hold components steady, whilst screws or nails are entered or glued joints dry.

Most types are available in a range of sizes and weights. Where size is quoted this generally indicates the maximum jaw opening or width.

A 'G' Cramps suitable for most general purpose applications, but care must be taken when used with wood that the cramp is not overtightened, thereby bruising the work. A softwood offcut placed between cramp and work will prevent this problem.

B Sliding bar type 'G' cramp similar to **A** but more versatile and quicker to adjust by a sliding bar arrangement. This type is often fitted with soft plastic caps to prevent damage to the work.

C Edge type 'G' cramp for simultaneous cramping

from two opposing directions, *see Fig. 1*. Ideal for cramping on edging strip to a large panel, such as a table top.

D Mitre cramp for holding a mitre joint steady whilst pinning. Used mainly for picture frame assembly, *Fig. 2*.

E Webbing type, consists of webbing fitted with a sliding buckle. Used for holding round and irregular shapes.

F Fitted bench, vice, a standard attachment for a woodworking bench.

G Portable bench vice, ideal for temporary attachment to a kitchen table or other makeshift work bench, *Fig. 3*. Various types are available, some with a range of interchangeable jaw linings.

H A sash cramp, normally used in pairs for holding

frames and wide panels together whilst glueing or fixing.

J A bench holdfast, designed as a permanent fixture to a woodworking bench and as a means of holding work flat to the bench top.

K A free standing portable bench and vice combination. Can be used to hold a wide range of items in all materials, from a small tube to a complete door.

Grinding and Honing Cutting Tools

A

D

B

'quenched' in water to prevent overheating and softening. Hand or electric drill powered grinders of this type are also suitable for this work. With any type of grinder, some form of eye protection should be either fitted to the machine or worn by the operator. For the home handyman without access to a grindstone, the work may be let out to a local contractor.

The angled edge only of the blade should be presented to the stone at the correct angle (normally 30°) for the tool, the thumb and forefinger being used to grip the blade and also to act as a 'stop' and 'steady' against the grindstone table. The right hand is then used to feed the blade squarely to the stone, *Fig. 2.*

The circular shape of the grindstone will produce a slightly hollow effect to the ground face; this is desirable as more honing re-sharpenings will be possible between re-grinding jobs.

Honing. The next stage of sharpening begins with an initial hone on a fine stone. For the home handyman a 225mm long combination stone of the type illustrated, **B**, is ideal.

The ground face of the blade must be brought squarely into contact with the face of the stone and at the correct angle for the tool (normally 25° to 30°). A simple tool for this work is the honing guide, **C**, which is used as *Fig. 1*. Use of the guide ensures an accurate and consistent angle to the honed face. Honing must be continued by rubbing the blade against the lightly oiled stone until a slight 'burr' of metal appears along the cutting edge. This 'burr' is removed by rubbing the blade *flat* to the fine side of the stone as *Fig. 3.* and **B**.

Gouges and other shaped cutting edges must be ground and honed on appropriately shaped stones. A typical 'slipstone' of this type is shown at **D** and *Fig. 4.*

The key to successful planing and chisel work lies in a really keen cutting edge to the tools, and to achieve this the plane iron or chisel must be carefully and correctly sharpened.

Grinding is the first stage in the sharpening process and can be carried out using an electric grinder such as that illustrated, **A**. When using a high speed machine of this type the blade being ground must be frequently

Screwdrivers

Screwdrivers form an important part of the home handyman's tool kit, and to cope with the range of screw sizes and types in use, a variety will be required.

There are two basic types of slots or 'keys' to screw heads. *Fig. 1* illustrates the common straight slotted type, widely used for fixing hinges, locks and other fittings in addition to general woodworking construction. *Fig. 2* illustrates the more modern cross slotted type which are these days being widely used, especially by manufacturers. The size of both types of slot vary with the size of the screw or bolt, and the first essential to safe and successful usage is a correct size matched screwdriver. Equally important is the condition of the screwdriver blade; it must be clean and accurately shaped to present a good fit to the screw slot, *Fig. 3*. A worn or incorrectly matched screwdriver presents a potential danger to the user because it can easily slip whilst under pressure.

When a screw is to be driven into wood, a correct size guide hole must first be drilled, *see Fig. 4*, consisting of a pilot hole for the screw threads, a clearance hole for the screw shank and a countersink for the screw head. The countersink will not be necessary when round head screws are being used. Special combination drill bits are available for drilling the

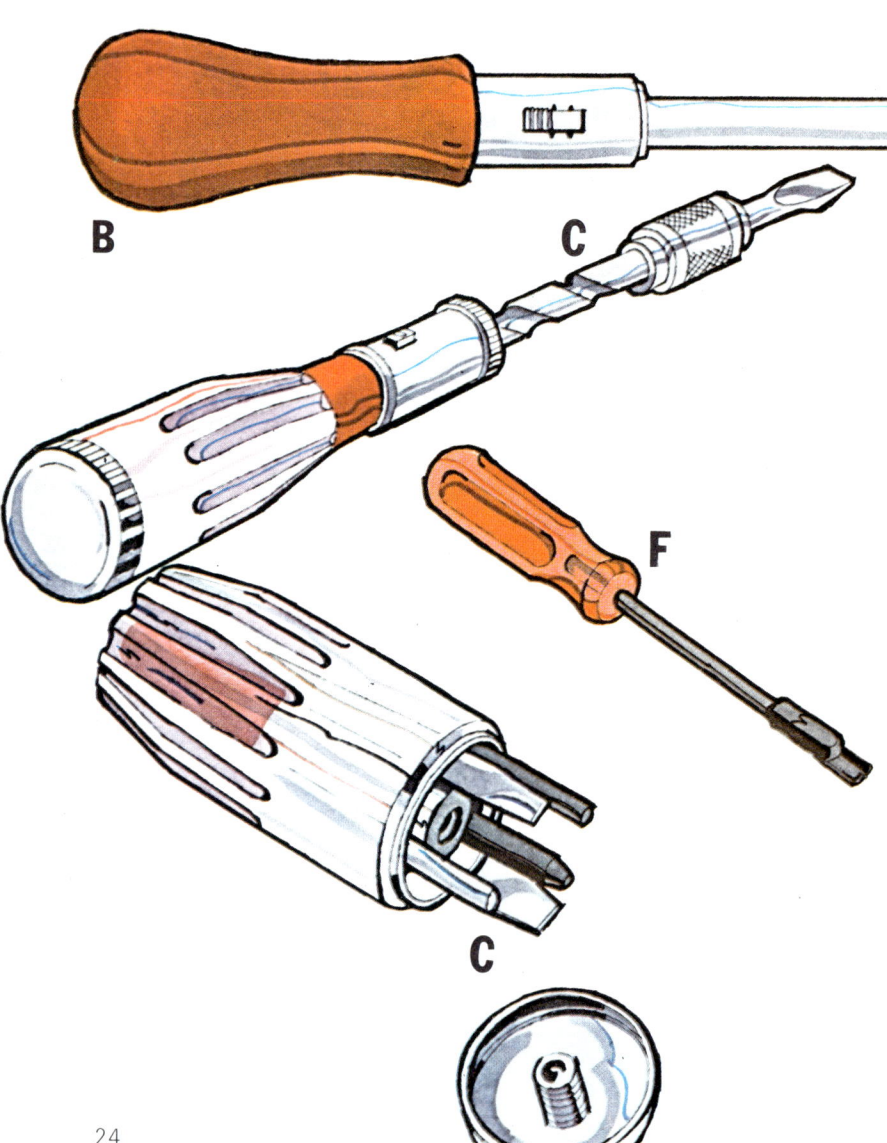

B

C

F

C

C

three holes in one operation — see 'Drills and Drilling', page 9.

Screwdrivers are available in an extremely wide range of sizes, shapes and types. Those illustrated represent a cross section able to cope with most home D.I.Y. jobs.

A A standard type of general purpose screwdriver, suitable for most medium size screws used for door hinges, woodwork assembly and so on.

B A ratchet type screwdriver suitable for lighter work, e.g. cabinet making and furniture construction.

C An automatic 'pump' type screwdriver, with an assortment of interchangeable screwdriving blades housed in the handle. This type of screwdriver, fitted with an appropriate bit, can also be used to drill holes, *see Fig. 5*. Operation for screwdriving or hole drilling is similar. One hand is used, as *Fig. 5*, to steady the chuck whilst palm pressure from the other hand is used to operate the spiral ratchet.

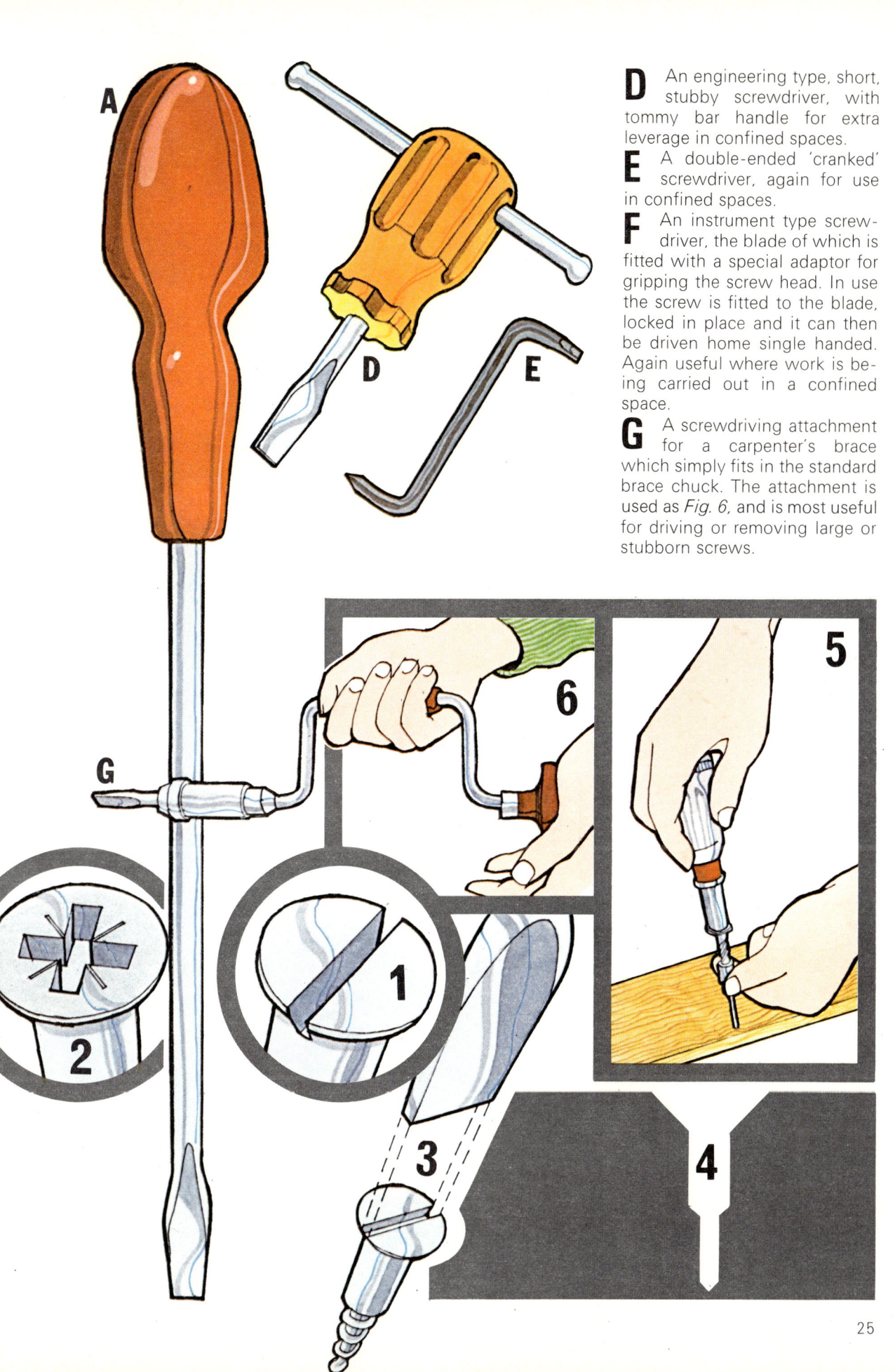

D An engineering type, short, stubby screwdriver, with tommy bar handle for extra leverage in confined spaces.

E A double-ended 'cranked' screwdriver, again for use in confined spaces.

F An instrument type screwdriver, the blade of which is fitted with a special adaptor for gripping the screw head. In use the screw is fitted to the blade, locked in place and it can then be driven home single handed. Again useful where work is being carried out in a confined space.

G A screwdriving attachment for a carpenter's brace which simply fits in the standard brace chuck. The attachment is used as *Fig. 6,* and is most useful for driving or removing large or stubborn screws.

Electric Drill
and
Attachments

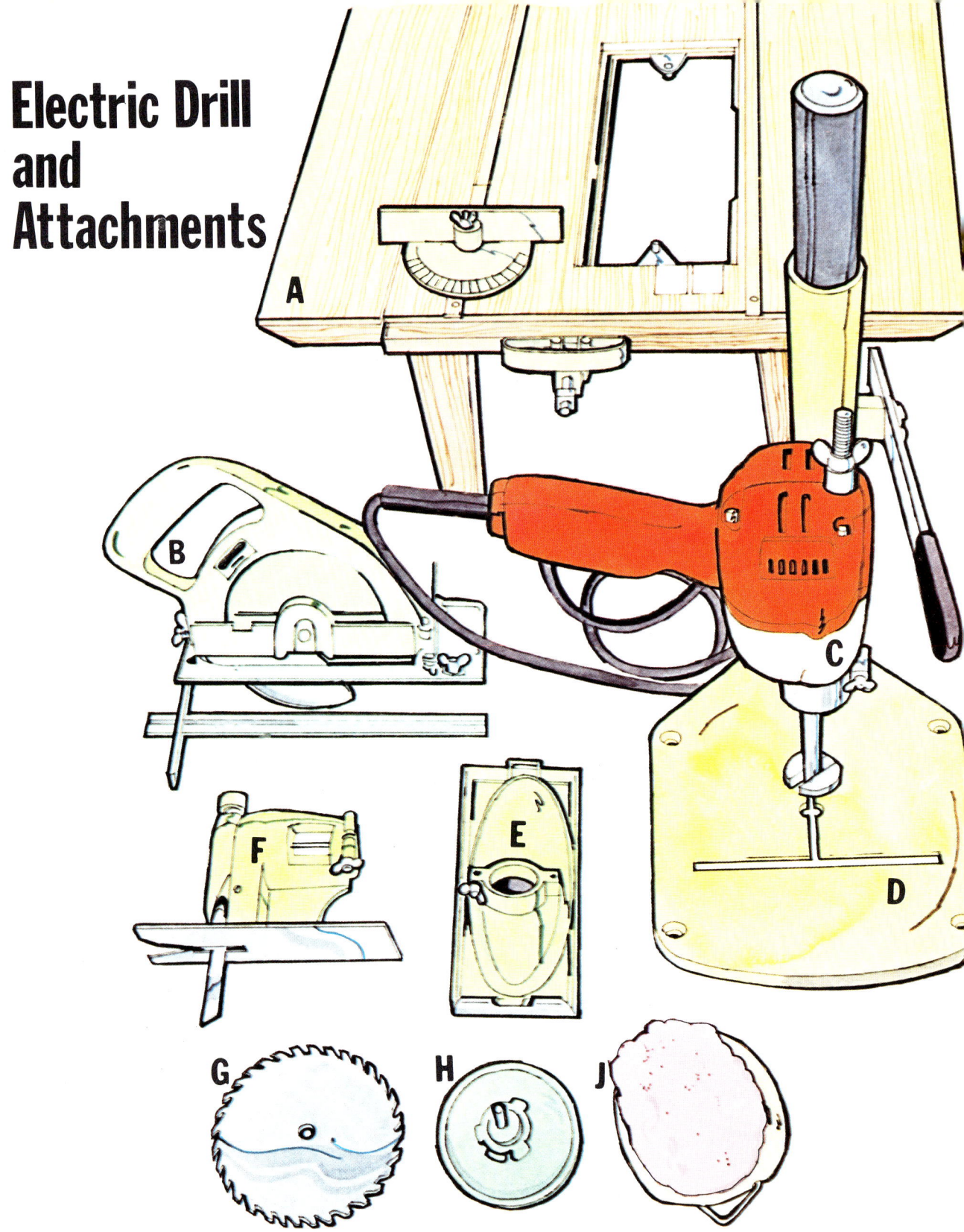

Most makes of standard electric drills can be used with a wide range of various types of purpose-made attachments. Some types of attachment, the disc sander for instance, are suitable for universal fitting to any make of drill, whilst other, more specialised, types should generally be matched to a specified type or make of drill.

Many modern drills are available fitted with an electrical or mechanical means of speed control. Generally the fast speed is best for woodwork and the slower speeds for drilling metal, masonry and glass. In addition some drills are also fitted with a percussion arrangement for drilling hard masonry.

Safety

An important point to bear in mind with all types of power tool is the potential danger of personal injury. Manufacturers' recommendations and usage instructions must always be carefully followed.

Drilling

The drill may be held as *Fig. 1* or fitted with a supplementary side handle as *Fig. 2*. Note that in *Fig. 1* the hands are kept well clear of the drill air cooling slots.

For complete accuracy and ease of operation the drill **C** can be fitted to a bench attachment **D**. Here the drill is firmly clamped in position and moved downward, for drilling, by hand pressure against an automatic return spring.

Sawing

The saw bench table **A** is designed to hold the drill-driven portable circular saw **B**, fitted with blade **G**. The bench is fitted with an adjustable fence and mitre guide for accurate ripping and cross-cutting. With most benches of this type the saw blade is also adjustable for cutting depth and may be used for grooving.

The drill-driven portable saw **B** is fitted with an adjustable side guide and is generally best used as *Fig. 3*. Note that both hands must be used to control the unit. For this reason it is vital that the material being worked is firmly cramped to a bench or trestle. With most makes the depth and angle of cut are adjustable. Sawing imposes a heavy strain on the drill motor and it is therefore important that the blade be kept sharp and the teeth correctly 'set'.

The rate of feed must also be carefully adjusted to allow the drill to run freely. Forcing the pace and straining the motor can quickly lead to damage through overheating.

The jig saw **F** fits to the front of the drill and works with a reciprocating action to the blade. The attachment can be used for cutting internal shapes, and blades are available for cutting metal and plastic in addition to wood.

Sanding

Two basic types of attachment cater for coarse and fine work. The orbital sander **E** is for fine finishing work, and the disc sander **H** used as *Fig. 2*, for more coarse work. The disc may also be fitted with a polishing mop **J**.

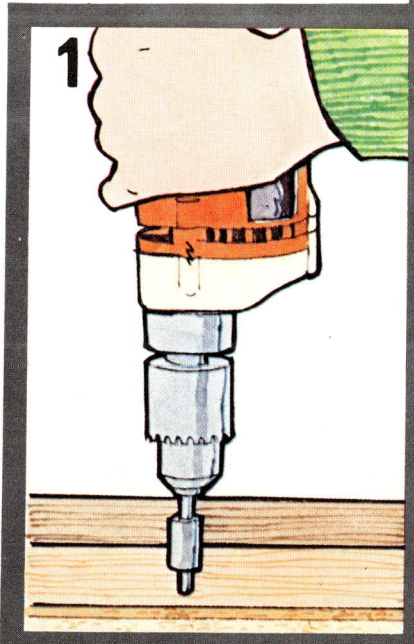

Self-Powered Tools

Self-powered woodworking tools and machines are generally intended to cope with heavier work than their drill-driven counterparts, and are therefore more suited to the experienced home woodworker equipped with a workshop. Most of the heavier tools tend to create considerable quantities of chips and dust, in addition to noise, and this is best kept away from the house.

An important aspect of using power tools is that of safety; the fast revolving blades and cutting edges must always be treated with respect and in all cases the tool manufacturers' instructions as to mounting, setting up and usage, especially in respect of safety guards, must be carefully followed.

A A radial arm circular saw. With this machine the blade, motor and much of the adjusting equipment is arranged to run in an overhead arm. When used for cross cutting, the material to be cut is held to the saw bench whilst the revolving blade is pulled across, *Fig. 1*. This method is much easier and safer for cross cutting long lengths of timber than would be possible with the standard bench type circular saw. In addition to simple cross cutting the angle of the blade or arm may be varied to produce angled or even compound angled cuts. In addition special blades and fittings are available for grooving and shaping. For rip sawing the blade may be set at right angles to the arm and the work fed to the blade. Much of the work possible

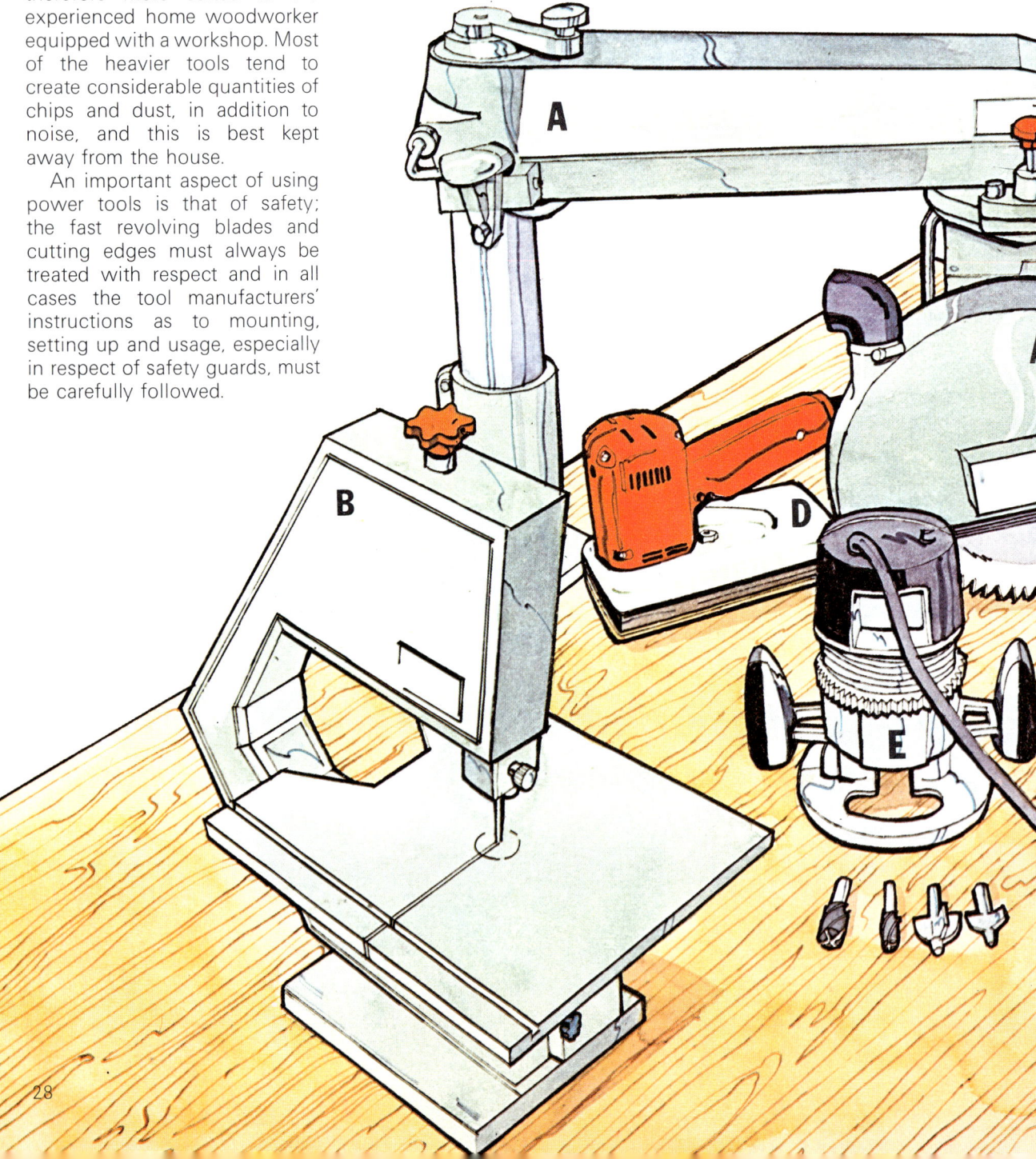

with this type of saw can also be done with a bench saw, but the latter is somewhat less versatile.

B A bench-mounted band saw, an ideal 'first' self-powered tool for the home workshop. Can be used to cross-cut or rip wood, metal or plastic, using the appropriate blade, and also for cutting curves and other intricate shapes, *see Fig. 2*. With most machines the cutting bench is adjustable to allow angled cuts to be made.

C A portable hand-held jig saw very versatile in use, especially for shaped cutting from sheet material and for cross cutting small section timber. Can be used for ripping but the blade tends to 'wander' with the wood grain making straight line cutting difficult. With most makes the saw platform can be adjusted to make angled cuts. The saw can be used for cutting metal or plastic when fitted with the appropriate blade.

D An orbital or finishing sander. Abrasive paper of varying grades is fitted to the sanding pad which is then driven with a fast rocking motion to produce a fine sanded finish to wood, metal or plastic surfaces. This tool allows finish sanding of large areas to be carried out accurately and quickly.

E A hand-held portable router. A high speed cutting machine which can be used to produce grooves, rebates and a complete range of other shapes quickly and accurately in both hard and softwood. In use, an appropriately shaped blade is fitted to the shaft of the machine and then brought into contact with the work, the shape of the fast revolving blade is then reproduced on the work. Accessories, such as the fence attachment, *see Fig. 3*, can be used to produce an accurate cut.

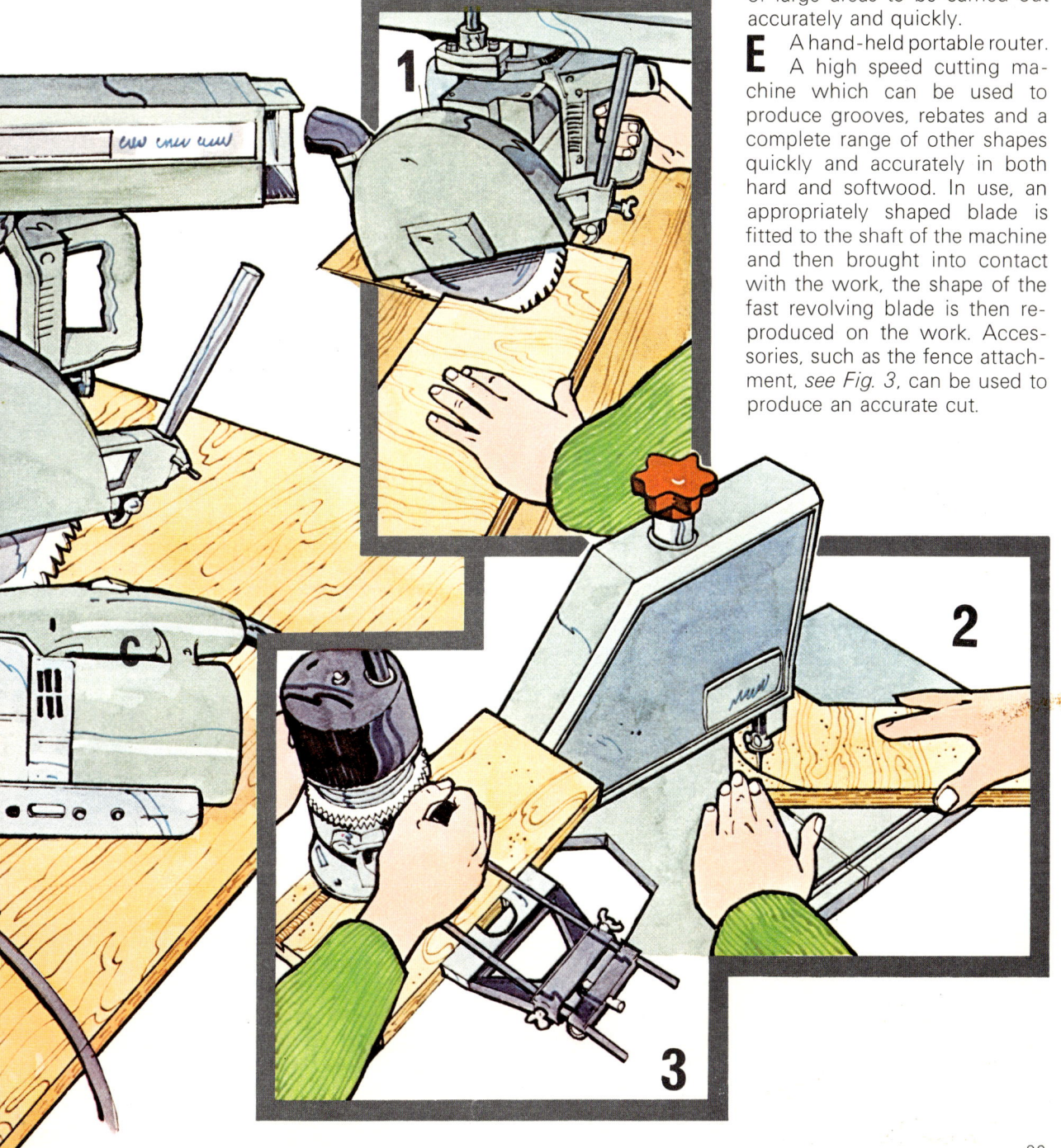

Hinges

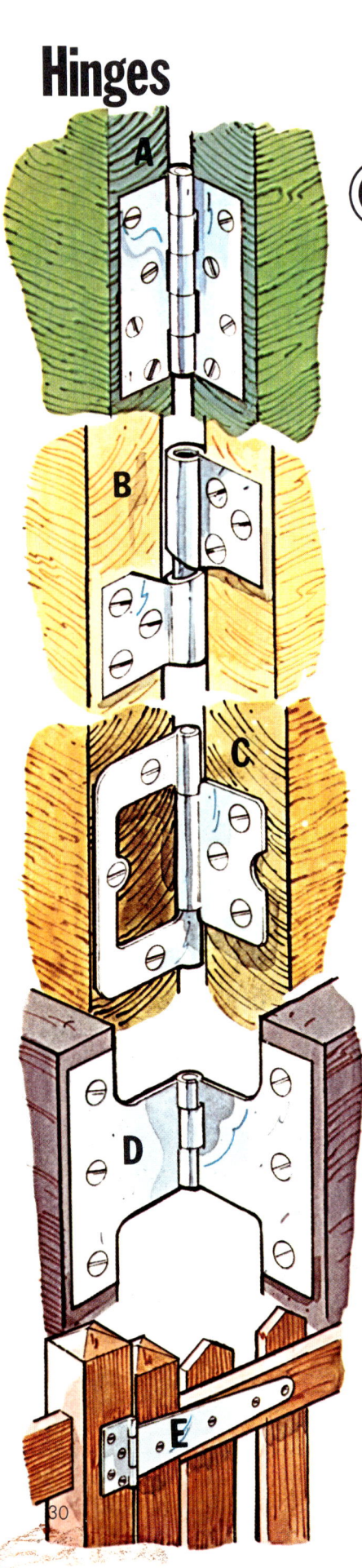

A lthough the range of hinges, catches and similar fittings is constantly growing, even to the stage of being somewhat confusing, the basic principles and methods of use remain much the same. Illustrated here are a cross-section of generally available styles and types which cover most home D.I.Y. applications. Hinges and most other fittings involve fixing screws, and much frustration and difficulty can be overcome if accurate pilot holes are pre-drilled in all cases.

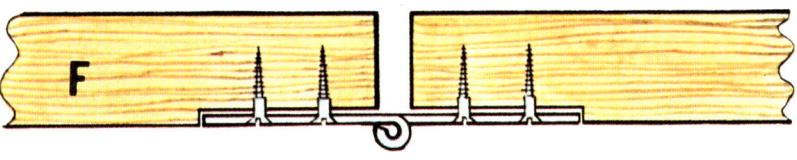

A An ordinary butt hinge as used for most house doors, but also available in a wide range of sizes and suitable for any flush fitting door. The standard hinge is made from pressed steel or moulded nylon but, where an extra heavy door is to be hung, either cast iron or brass butt hinges should be used. Small sizes are also available in cast brass for use in quality cabinet making. Fitting this type of hinge can present a problem to the inexperienced woodworker, because an accurate recess must first be chiselled in both door and frame, for the hinge tongues.

B A pin type rising butt. The central part of the hinge has a built-in slope to the mating surfaces which cause the door to rise as it is opened. Intended for use on internal house doors to provide ground clearance for carpets and other floor coverings. Fitted in a similar manner and often used as a

replacement for **A**.

C A flush or hurlhinge, again available in a range of sizes to suit house or cabinet doors. Easier to fit that **A** or **B** because frame or door recess slots are not necessary.

D A stand-off or parliament hinge. Again generally used for full sized house door or window shutters, and designed to clear any frame surround to allow opening through a complete 180°.

E 'T' hinge as used for a garden gate, shed doors or tool box. Standard types are made from pressed steel but decorative and heavy duty types are often made from cast iron or steel bar.

F A back flap hinge, similar in appearance to **A** but with wider tongues. Generally used as illustrated for a hinged flap or similar application. Where a superior finish is required for this type of application, a pair of cast brass counter top hinges could

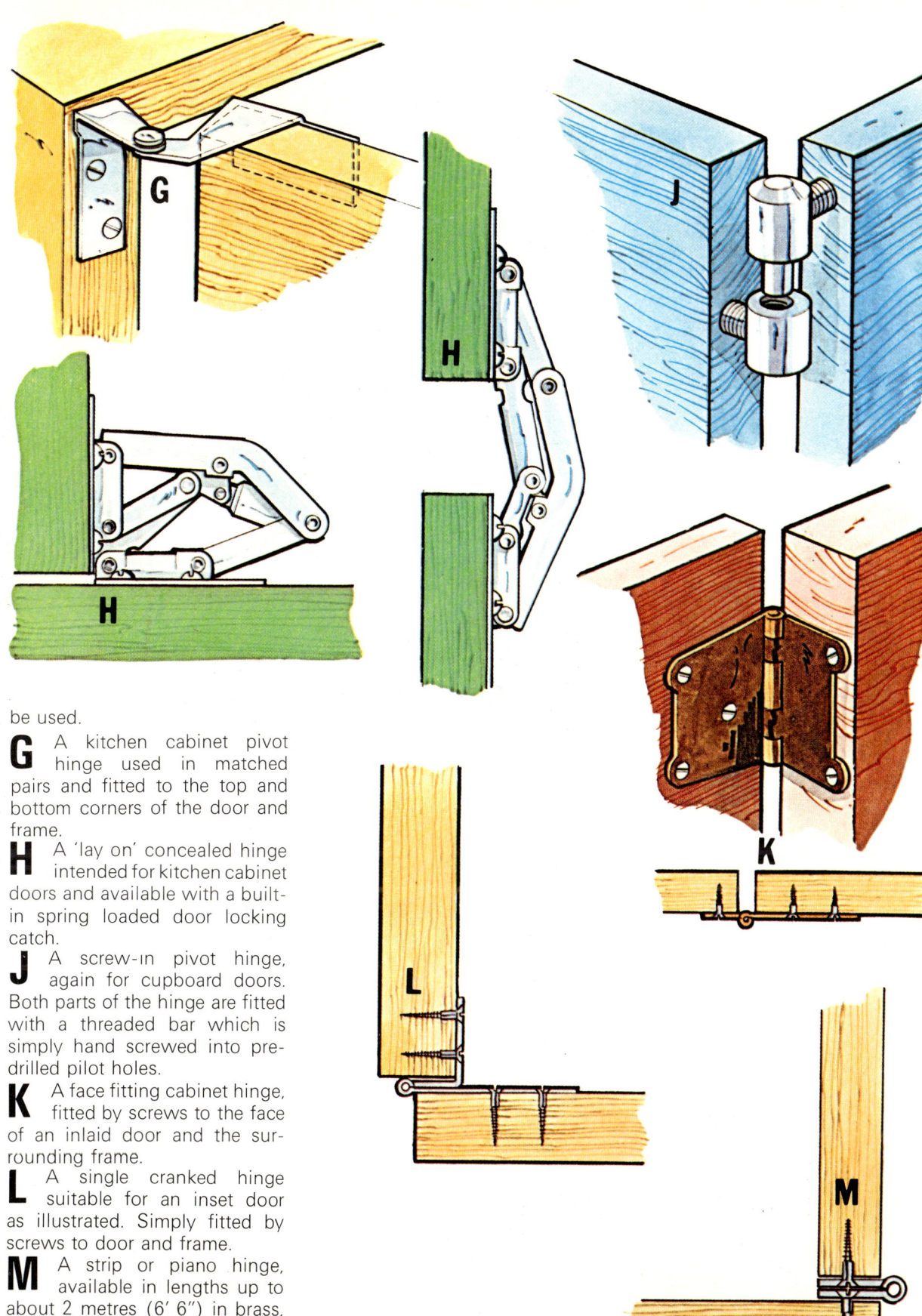

be used.

G A kitchen cabinet pivot hinge used in matched pairs and fitted to the top and bottom corners of the door and frame.

H A 'lay on' concealed hinge intended for kitchen cabinet doors and available with a built-in spring loaded door locking catch.

J A screw-in pivot hinge, again for cupboard doors. Both parts of the hinge are fitted with a threaded bar which is simply hand screwed into pre-drilled pilot holes.

K A face fitting cabinet hinge, fitted by screws to the face of an inlaid door and the surrounding frame.

L A single cranked hinge suitable for an inset door as illustrated. Simply fitted by screws to door and frame.

M A strip or piano hinge, available in lengths up to about 2 metres (6' 6") in brass, steel or plastic. Generally best fitted to the full length of a door.

Locks and Catches

The various types of locks and catches available are designed to perform specific functions. Illustrated are some of the basic types:

A A standard night type latch as fitted to many house front doors. Full fitting instructions and a drilling template are supplied with the lock.

B Standard type rimlock as fitted to many house rear doors. Both lock and catch are simply screwed to the inner door and frame face.

C Mortise type lock normally fitted to doors with locks **A** or **B** as additional security. In fitting, the lock is mortised into the door edge.

D A padlock and hasp used mainly for securing a garden shed or workshop or large tool box.

E A self closing garden gate latch.

F A box lock; here the main part of the lock is fixed to the box side and the catch plate fixed to the lid. A bolt in the lock

snaps through the catch plate slots when the key is operated. Normally used on light sewing and trinket or jewel boxes.

G A simple cupboard door lock fitted to the inner face of the door. The lock tongue locks into a slot cut into the cupboard side or frame.

H A drawer lock, similar to the box lock but recessed into the rear face of the drawer front.

J A simple ball catch, available in a range of sizes to suit small cupboard or full sized room doors. Fitted by drilling a hole in the door edge and then recessing for the face plate. The catch plate is recessed into the door frame.

K A magnetic catch, available in a range of sizes and magnetic strength to suit most sizes of cupboard door.

L A nylon roller catch for cupboard doors. Has the advantage of being self centering and will therefore hold the closed door neat and level.

Screws

Using the appropriate nail, screw or bolt can often considerably simplify a job in addition to ensuring optimum strength. Size choice is also important and should be carefully matched to the work in hand.

Screws

A, B, C and **E:** standard woodworking screws.

D: alternative head slot for *A, B and C.*

F: Mirror or dome head.

G, H, J: screw head cups.

K: spanner driven coach screw.

L: dowel type for edge jointing.

M: screw hook.

N: screw bolt.

Bolts

A: woodworking coach bolt.

B: swing hook.

C: rag bolt for bedding in concrete.

D: wall bolt.

E: galvanised gutter bolt.

F, G, H and **J:** machine screws with varying head patterns.

Nuts

A: standard 'full' nut.

B: half or lock nut.

C: domed type.

D: nylon insert lock nut.

E: hand-tightened wing nut.

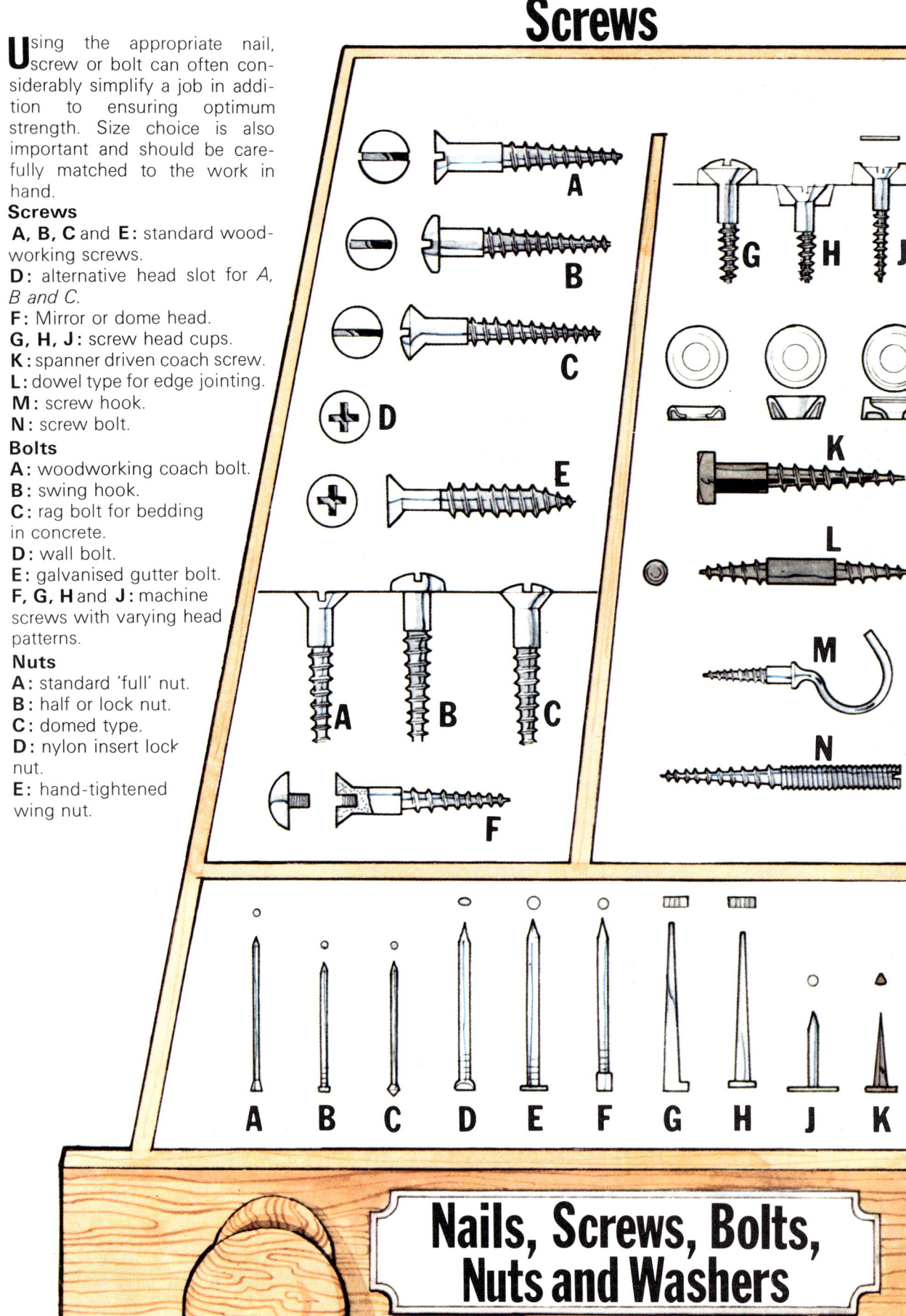

Nails, Screws, Bolts, Nuts and Washers

Bolts Nuts and Washers

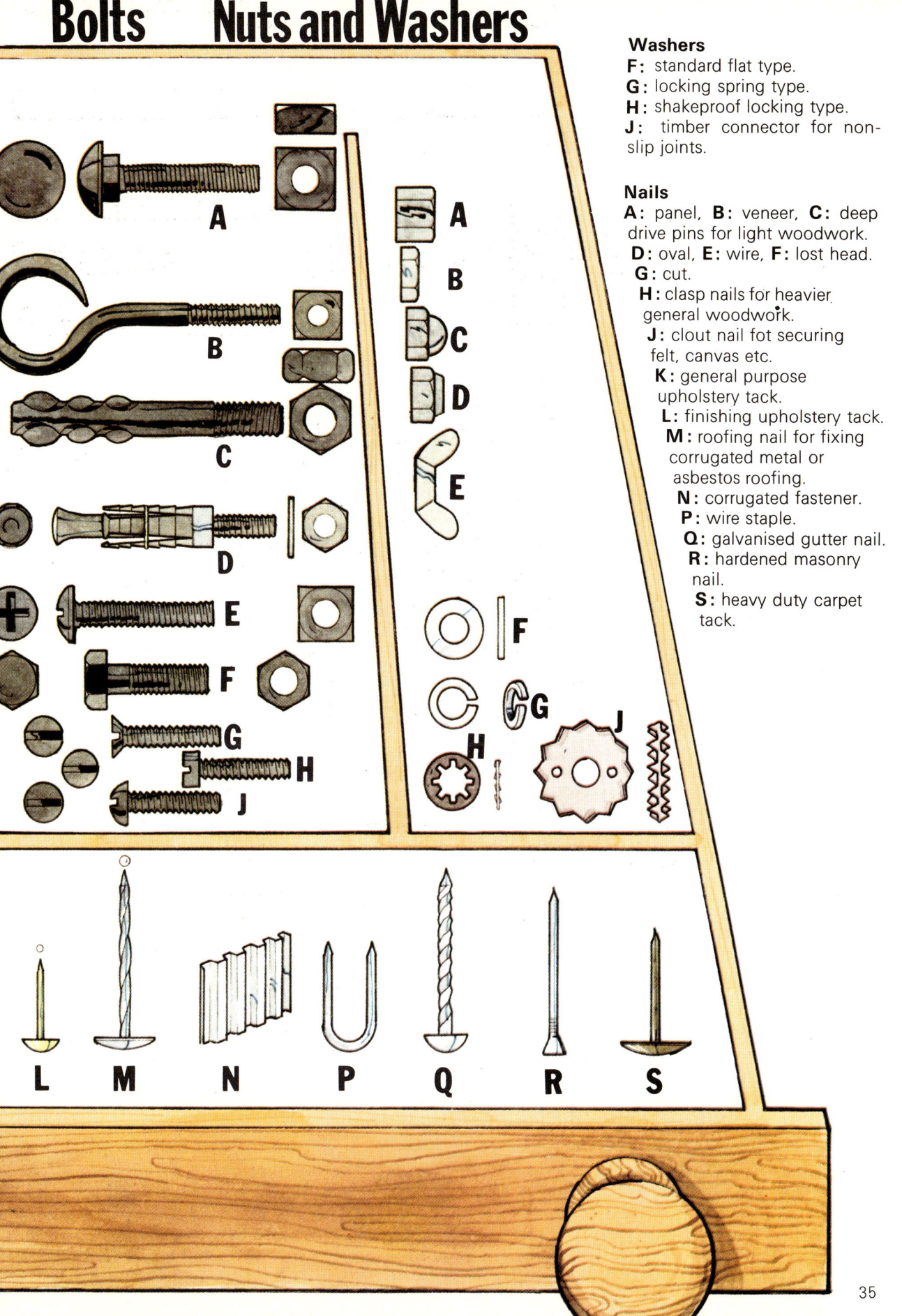

Wall Fixings

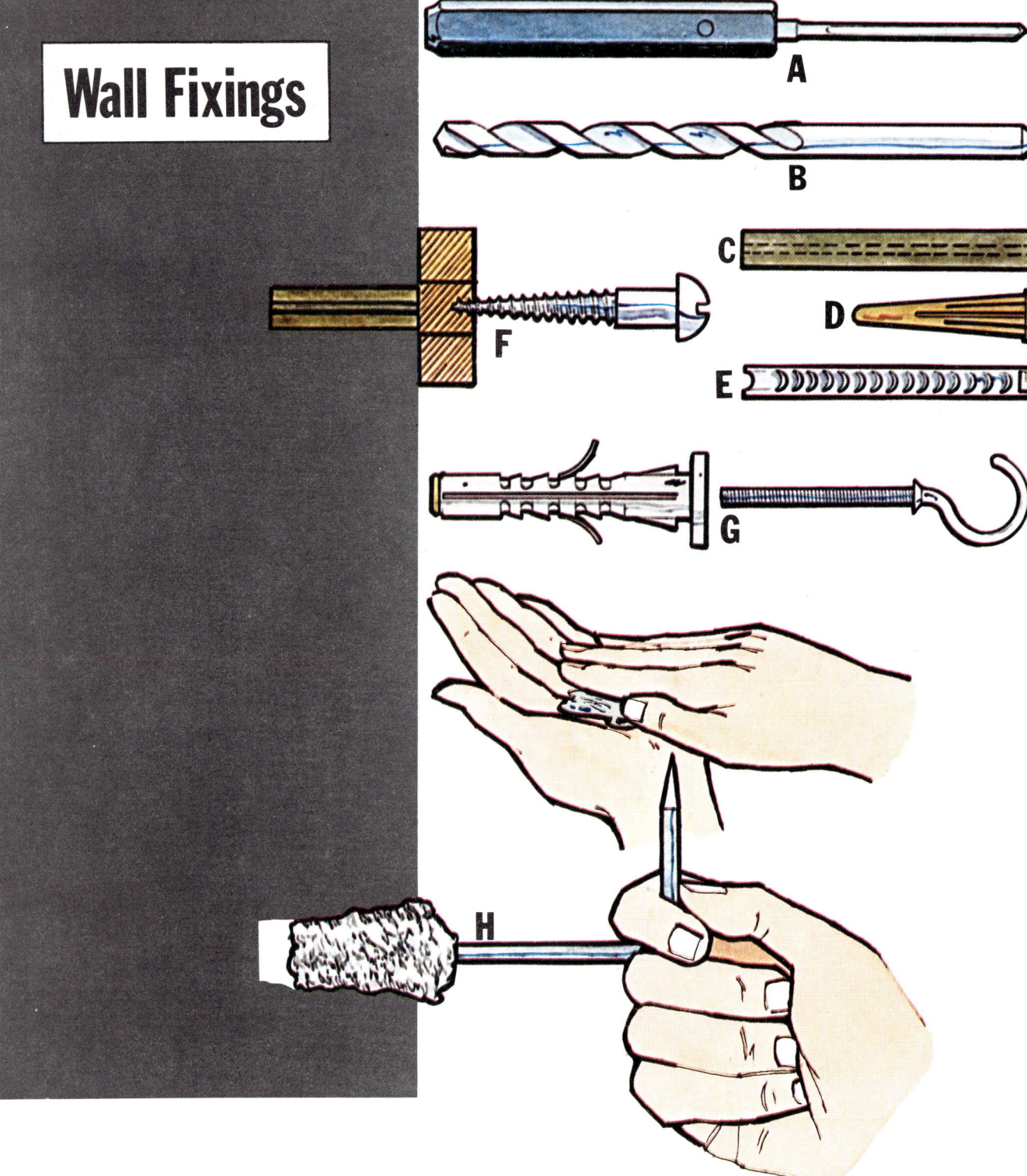

The secret of safe wall fixing lies in using the appropriate fitting.

Solid Walls

A: a hammer-driven boring chisel with interchangeable blades of different sizes.

B: a purpose-made masonry bit for drilling holes in all types of masonry.

C: a fibre type wall plug.

D: a plastic wall plug.

E: a soft metal wall plug.

All used as **F** by pressing into a correctly size matched hole; as a screw is entered the plug is expanded to grip the surrounding masonry.

G: a threaded cup hook used in a similar manner to **F**, but here plug expansion is by the threaded part of the hook pulling a tapered metal insert into the end of the wall plug.

H: illustrates a special compound filler, ideal for use in a ragged or mis-shapen hole. In use the compound is slightly dampened before being compressed into the hole. A screw, driven into the compound, causes it to expand.

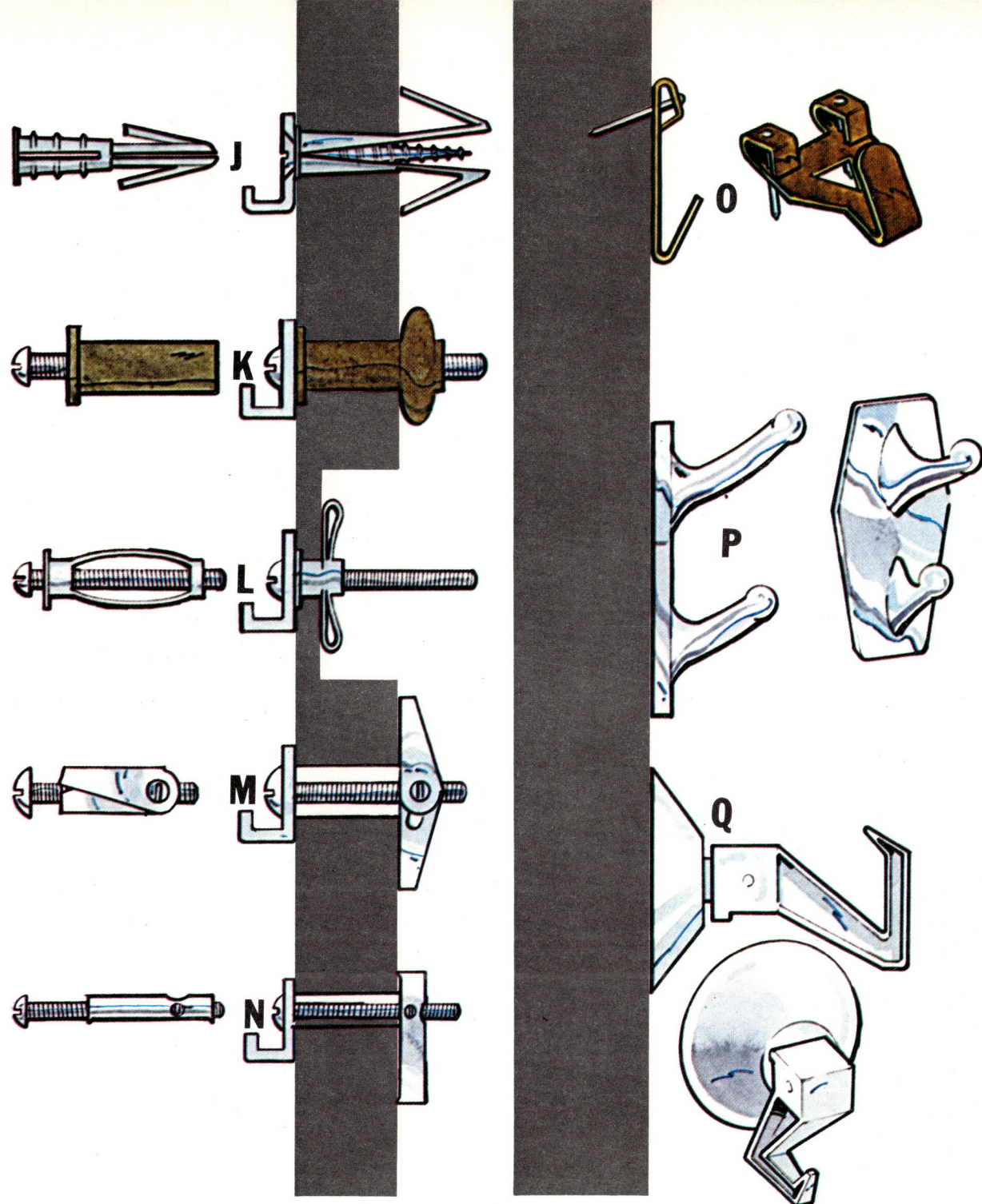

Hollow Walls

Hollow walls may be clad with any one of a range of materials including wood, asbestos, hardboard, or plasterboard, and a drill appropriate to the material should be used.

J: a plastic plug type fixing with flexible 'legs' which spring apart in the wall cavity.

K: a rubber sleeve type which expands as the fixing screw is tightened

L: a collapsible wall anchor.

M: the spring loaded 'wings' of this fitting fly apart inside the wall cavity.

N: a gravity toggle fixing. Here a pivoted bar falls away from the fixing screw inside the wall cavity.

Universal Types

O: a wall picture hook fixed by driving the hardened metal pins in with a hammer.

P: a self-adhesive coat hook, stuck directly to the wall after removal of the protective paper.

Q: a suction cup type where levering the hook downward evacuates air from an internal wall fitted suction cup.

Adhesives

The adhesives and uses listed opposite may be used as a general guide for most home D.I.Y. projects and repairs. However, with the range and types of products constantly being marketed, recommendations suggested are always subject to individual manufacturers' instructions.

In addition to the types mentioned, many specialised adhesives are available for such jobs as fixing floor, wall and ceiling tiles, mosaics, wall coverings of various types, boat building and so on. Here it is important that manufacturers' or suppliers' advice be sought at time of purchase to ensure that a correct adhesive is used. In addition to the type of material and fixing surface, exposure to dampness, heat or weather are also important considerations.

Using the Adhesive

Having established the correct type of adhesive for the job in hand, check carefully the manufacturers' recommendations as to use. Many adhesives are, for instance, affected by extremes of temperature; indeed a minimum and maximum storage temperature is often necessary to avoid deterioration. Generally, low temperature or excessive humidity will slow the drying time, whilst high temperature will speed it up. In either case the finished joint may be weakened if conditions exceed those recommended.

Surface Preparation

Generally, surfaces to be joined must be clean and free from dust, grease, or dirt, and must be dry, although with some adhesives, *cyanoacrylates* for instance, damping is suggested to prevent absorption of the adhesive.

In many applications the mating surfaces must be 'keyed' to provide effective grip for the adhesive. This is especially important where non-absorbent surfaces are involved. Here an abrasive material, i.e. glass paper, emery cloth, wire wool, should be used to lightly roughen the surface and provide the necessary 'key'.

Where a previously glued or painted surface is to be joined, then the old glue or paint should be scraped away to solid backing.

Cramping (See Cramps and Cramping, pages 20–21.)

Depending on the type of adhesive, or application, cramping of the mating parts may be necessary. Pressure should be sufficient to hold the joint firmly but not to the extent where too much glue is squeezed away.

Drying (or Curing) Time

The adhesive must be left to thoroughly harden for the recommended period, bearing in mind of course any change due to excessive temperature or humidity. No load should be imposed during the drying period. For maximum strength, drying time should not be accelerated by heat beyond the manufacturers' instructions.

Animal (Scotch Glue)	wood, paper, cardboard, hardboard, chipboard	Supplied ready to use in a tube, or in solid form requiring heating prior to use. Now generally superseded by PVA or synthetic adhesives.
PVA	wood, paper, cardboard, hardboard, chipboard, fabric, some types suitable for bonding cement work, expanded polystyrene etc.	Supplied ready to use in, generally, soft plastic squeezy type containers. Suitable for most home woodworking and similar jobs that are not subject to extra heavy stress or exposure to damp.
Synthetic Resin	wood, chipboard, hardboard	Generally supplied in powder form for mixing with water immediately prior to use. Has a limited 'mixed' life, widely used for joinery and woodwork.
Contact Adhesive	plastic laminate, wood, leather, some fabrics, rigid PVC, cork, rubber, metal, hardboard, chipboard, plasterboard	Supplied ready to use in tin or tube. After spreading to both mating surfaces must be left until dry before final surface alignment and contact. Generally used for bonding plastic laminate, rigid sheet wall panels and other large areas. Not suitable for use in extremes of heat or dampness.
Cellulose (Balsa Cement)	wood, china, glass	Supplied ready to use in a tube. Widely used for model making with balsa wood. Also suitable for repair to china, and glass, ornaments. Very quick drying.
General purpose	most household materials, except expanded polystyrene and polythene	Supplied ready for use in a tube. Suitable for small repair jobs around the house and workshop.
Polystyrene cement	plastics (other than expanded polystyrene)	Supplied ready for use in a tube. Used mainly for assembling plastic model and similar kits.
Latex and rubber types	fabrics, carpets, soft leather	Supplied ready for use in tubes or tins. Suitable for use with fabrics, lampshade making, carpet binding etc. where a soft, flexible joint is required.
Epoxy resin	wood, metal, glass, stone, crockery, pottery, rigid plastics	Supplied as a resin and hardener in separate containers, which, after mixing, is ready for use. Especially suitable where two unlike materials are to be joined.
PVC	flexible PVC	Supplied ready for use in tins or tubes and suitable for repairing flexible PVC. May cause some materials to distort and it is advisable to check a 'test' area for reaction.
Cyano-acrylate (Contact cement)	metal, glass, plastics, hardwood	Supplied ready for use in a tube. Suitable for bonding most materials where a good surface contact is possible. A solid bond is obtained almost instantaneously.

Woodworking Joints 1

To many home handyman the term 'woodworking joints' can be off-putting, bringing to mind complicated dovetailed and similar specialised work. In point of fact woodworking joints for many projects do not need to be complicated and in most cases something considerably less specialised than a dovetail will prove perfectly adequate.

1 Straight Overlap, 2 Butt (with or without reinforcing battens) and **3 Overlap**, all simple joints suitable where strength is more important than appearance. Fixing may be with nails, screws, or bolts and glue.

4 Flush Butt, held together initially with a corrugated fastener and then covered with a sheet material such as plywood or hardboard.

5 Dowelled. A neat and strong *secret* type joint. Purpose made jigs are available to ensure accurate drilling. Grooves must be cut along the length of the dowels to prevent glue pressure build-up as the joint is forced home.

6 Flush Butt. Similar to *4*, but reinforced with metal brackets.

fig 1

5

6

7

7 Flush Bolted. Ideal for a joint that will be frequently dismantled and assembled.

8, 9, 10. All variations of the **Half Lap** joint, which are neat in appearance and of good strength. *Figs. 1* and *2* illustrate the method of cutting and chiselling this type of joint.

11 Bridle. Similar to the half lap but can be fixed using glue only.

8

9

10

11

fig 2

41

Woodworking Joints 2

12 **Mortise & Tenon.** A strong neat joint used in carpentry and cabinet making, where both strength and neatness of appearance are important. With this type of joint accurate marking and cutting is essential. Mark the mortise (the *female* part of the joint) to no more than $\frac{1}{3}$ the width of the timber and then chisel to shape after drilling to the full width – *Fig. 3*. Cut back the ends of the mortise sufficiently to accommodate the fixing wedges. Next mark the tenon and cut as *Fig. 1* and *4*. Assemble after applying glue, cramping where possible, then tap home the fixing wedges.

13 **Rebate.** Useful for corner joints where fairly wide

12

fig 3

fig 4

panels are used. Using either a hand or power saw, an initial cut is made parallel to the end of the panel and to the depth and width of the rebate. Surplus material is then removed using a chisel as *Fig. 5*. Fixing is generally by glue and panel pins as shown, but the pins may be driven through the uncut member where a deep rebate is used.

14 **Groove & Rebate.** Suitable for use in similar situations to the ordinary rebate but can be fixed by glue only. Two parallel cuts are made to either side of the groove using a hand or power saw. The central waste material is then chiselled away as *Fig. 5*. The rebate is cut as described.

15 **Scarf.** A simple method of end jointing two pieces of timber. Suitable only where strength is not important or where the joint is reinforced by fixing to a solid adjacent surface. Often used for the in-situ repair of wooden door and window frames where the bottom or corner has rotted. Fixing is by skew nailing as shown.

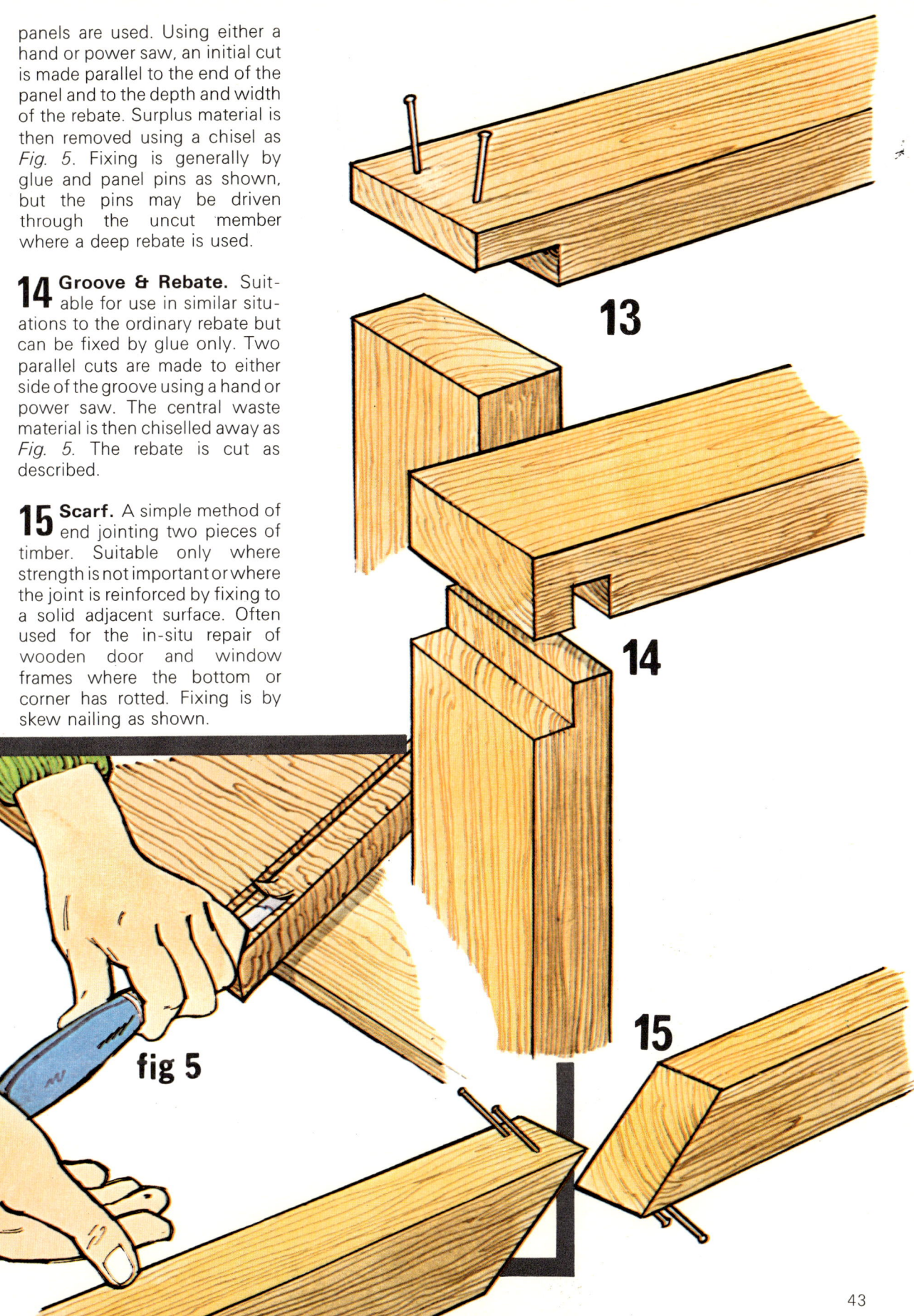

13

14

fig 5

15

Woodworking Joints 3

16 The Housing Joint

A simple but useful joint where a neat and strong 'T' connection is required between two rectangular section timbers. This type of joint is frequently used in the construction of bookcases and other shelved storage units as a means of joining the shelves to the side vertical members.

Having marked the area to be cut away, check for complete accuracy by laying the board to be jointed between the marks. Use a tenon saw and bench stop, *Fig. 1*, to make two saw cuts across the board and to the depth of the cut. If the grain of the wood is twisted or knotty, then make a further full depth cut to the centre of the marks. The central area is pared away with a chisel, *Fig. 2*, with the board either firmly held in a vice or on a bench stop. The centre part of the joint should be very slightly undercut to ensure good contact at the visible ends. Fixing can be by nails or screws, or where the joint is part of a complete unit, by glueing and cramping.

17 The Stopped Housing Joint

This joint is used in much the same way as the through hous-

fig 6

18 The Comb Joint

The comb joint provides a strong means of making a right angle corner joint. It is especially useful where two unlike materials, for instance solid wood and plywood, are to be jointed. The joint is often used where strength is more important than appearance.

The joint can be cut by hand using a tenon and coping saw in much the same way as the dovetail joint, *Figs. 9 and 10*, but where a number have to be cut, a purpose made circular saw bench attachment can be usefully employed. Fixing is normally by glue only.

19 Grooved and Tongued Edge Joint

A joint normally used where lengths or panels of timber need to be accurately and strongly edge-jointed. The grooves may be cut with a portable circular saw, *Fig. 7*, or with a combination plane, after the edges have been planed true and matched, see Planes and Planing, page 18. For maximum strength the tongue should be cut from plywood. Fixing is by glueing and cramping.

ing joint but has the advantage of a neater frontal appearance and is often used for intermediate shelves in a well-built bookcase. Again accurate marking is essential and the *female* part of the joint, *Fig. 6*, should be cut first. Use a tenon saw to make two sloping cuts to the sides of the housing and then cut around the end, using a chisel and mallet as *Fig. 6*. The central area is next pared away with the chisel and the end cuts progressively deepened.

With the housing neatly cut, the horizontal member can be slid in position and the depth of the frontal cut out accurately marked. Fixing can be by any of the methods described.

fig 7

Woodworking Joints 4

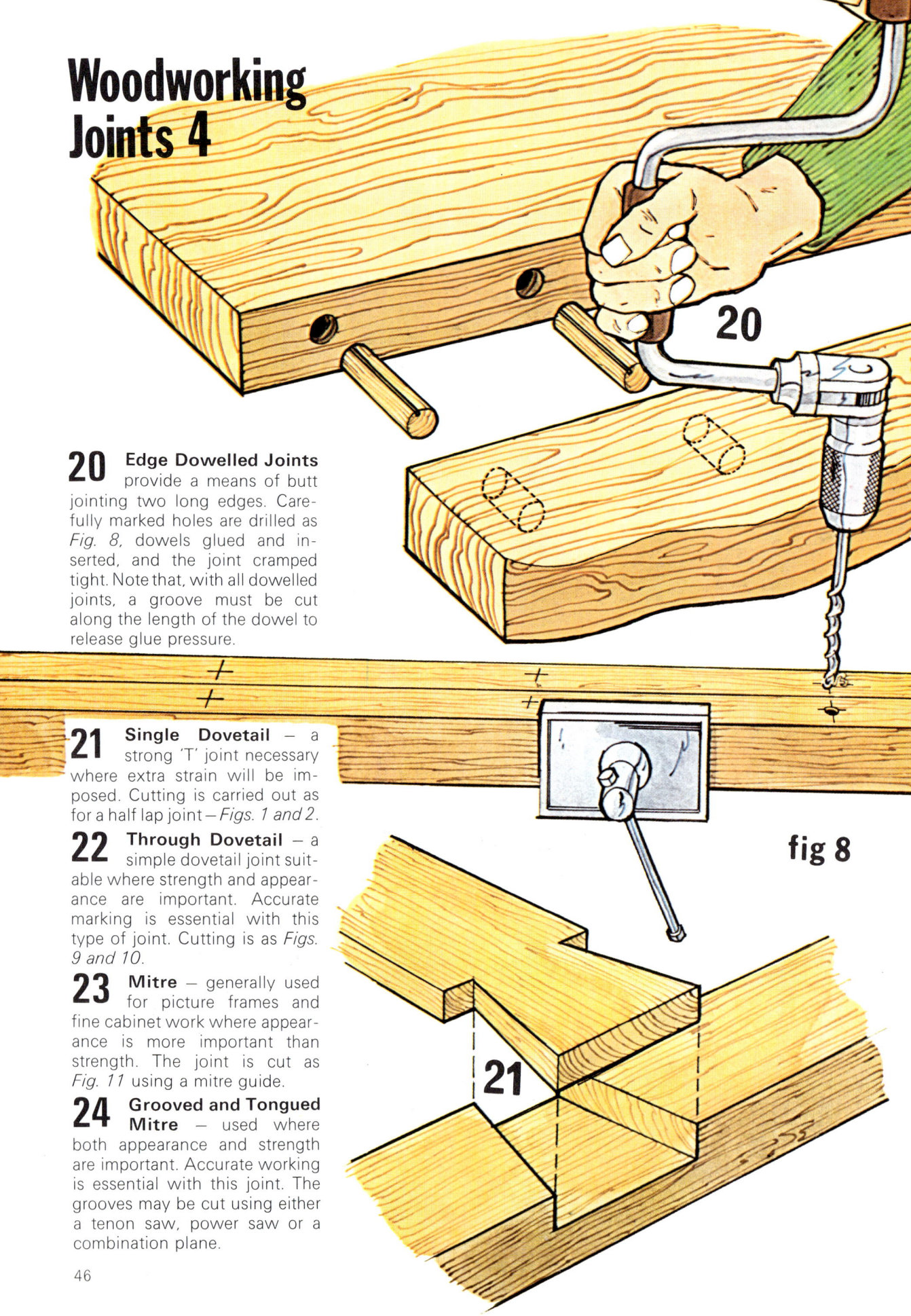

20 **Edge Dowelled Joints** provide a means of butt jointing two long edges. Carefully marked holes are drilled as *Fig. 8*, dowels glued and inserted, and the joint cramped tight. Note that, with all dowelled joints, a groove must be cut along the length of the dowel to release glue pressure.

20

fig 8

21 **Single Dovetail** — a strong 'T' joint necessary where extra strain will be imposed. Cutting is carried out as for a half lap joint — *Figs. 1 and 2*.

22 **Through Dovetail** — a simple dovetail joint suitable where strength and appearance are important. Accurate marking is essential with this type of joint. Cutting is as *Figs. 9 and 10*.

23 **Mitre** — generally used for picture frames and fine cabinet work where appearance is more important than strength. The joint is cut as *Fig. 11* using a mitre guide.

24 **Grooved and Tongued Mitre** — used where both appearance and strength are important. Accurate working is essential with this joint. The grooves may be cut using either a tenon saw, power saw or a combination plane.

21

22

fig 9

fig 10

23

24

fig 11

Planning

Whatever type of building project is to be tackled, initial work must be concerned with careful planning. For all but very simple jobs, notes should be made of the stages of work involved, the materials and tools required, and whether advice or assistance of an expert or specialised contractor is necessary. A schedule of work can then be drawn up and an estimate, of cost and time involved, arrived at. In this way many unforeseen problems can be brought to light and overcome before work is under way.

Basically planning means having all necessary tools, materials and help available as and when required, and working in an organised and practical way.

Woodwork and Furniture
Timber and sheet material is available in standard sizes and, where possible, woodworking projects should be designed around these. In this way, unnecessary cutting and waste can be reduced to a minimum and much time and cost saved against using specially prepared sizes.

Solid Wood
Solid wood is generally available in various timber species in a range of sectional sizes as either sawn or 'prepared' (planed all round). The stated size of solid timber refers to the size before planing, a process which often reduces size by between 3 mm ($\frac{1}{8}$ in) and 6 mm ($\frac{1}{4}$ in). Where sectional size is critical it is as well to visit the yard of the timber supplier and check measurements against those quoted.

Soft wood is also generally available in standard 'moulded' shapes and sizes for use as skirting board, architrave, glazing bar and so on. Hàrd woods are available in more delicate mouldings for edge finishing, picture frames and the like. Again, at the planning stage, details of sizes

and shapes readily available should be checked, and, where possible, incorporated with the work.

Joinery
Ready-made doors, windows and other frames are kept by larger timber yards as stock items. A wide range of types and sizes are available, and purchasing 'ready-made' in this way is generally more economical overall than home-built joinery.

Sheet Materials
Sheet materials such as hardboard, chipboard, plywood and blockboard, are generally available in standard sizes of 2440 mm (8 ft) × 1220 mm (4 ft), some suppliers, however, stock smaller sheet sizes. Plywood, chipboard and blockboard, in addition to the basic raw finish, can also be purchased with various facings from veneered timber to melamine and simulated wood grains. Hardboard is available with a pre-finished enamelled surface.

Veneered chipboard panels have become increasingly popular over recent years as a result of the decline in quality and availability of solid wood.

Panels are generally available in lengths up to 2440 mm (8 ft) and in widths from about 75 mm (3 in) in 75 mm (3 in) increments up to 1220 mm (4 ft) with both long edges veneered. Where this type of panel is to be used a manufacturer's stock size list should be consulted as a reference at the planning stage.

Where standard width panels cannot be specified throughout it may be possible to cut down one standard panel to provide two to the size required. For instance, a 230 mm (9 in) width could be cut down to provide two non-standard 115 mm ($4\frac{1}{2}$ in) wide panels. Most veneered board manufacturers also market an easily fixed matching edge trim which can then be used to cover the cut edges.

Fittings and Fixings
Screws, nails, hinges, catches and similar fittings come in an ever-increasing range of styles and types. Some are suitable for general purpose application, whilst others are designed to cope with one or two special applications. At the planning stage, full information should be gathered to see that the most suitable part is specified and used.

Building Work
When building work and structural alterations are under consideration, an early enquiry should be made of the local authority Surveyor's office in order to settle the question of official approval for the work. A verbal enquiry, preferably accompanied by a sketch or drawing, often proves helpful in the first instance and can often save much time in the long term.

An important point to bear in mind with building work is that of design and safety standards. Here professional planning will generally be required, in order to produce a sound and stable structure which complies with all regulations and standard codes of practice.

49

Working with Plastic Laminate

Plastic laminate veneer such as Formica, Arborite etc., is a versatile material which can be used to great advantage by the home handyman. The storage unit project described on pages 52–54 is designed around laminate, and serves as an illustration of how a professional finish can easily be achieved using cheap material and a simple butt-jointed construction.

As with all materials, techniques of cutting and working must be practised before a full project is tackled. Most D.I.Y. shops now sell laminate in small sheet or off-cut sizes, which are ideal for this purpose. Once the basic methods of cutting, bonding and trimming have been mastered, the range of possible usage is endless.

Laminate is generally available in a range of full sheet and cut sizes up to about 3050 mm (10 ft) × 1220 mm (4 ft). Most manufacturers also market a matching flexible strip approximately 25 mm (1 in) wide as an edging material suitable for straight or curved surfaces.

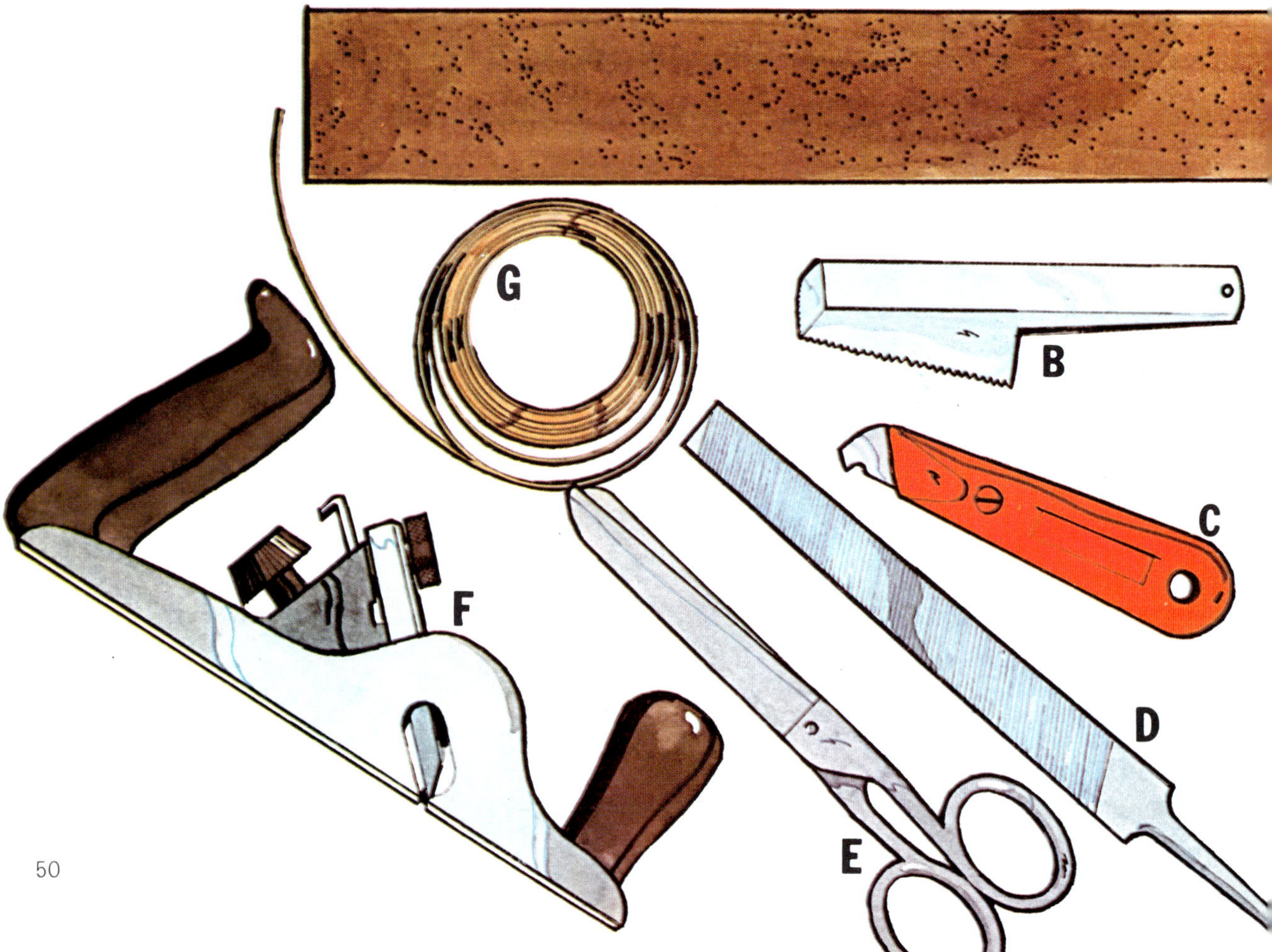

Cutting

The simplest method of cutting is to use a hardboard or ply straight edge, **A**, in conjunction with a scoring type laminate cutter **C**. The laminate to be cut must be laid on a clean, flat surface. Small sheets can be cut on a bench but larger sheets are best laid on a hardboard panel on the floor. Lay the laminate finished side up and mark the line to be cut with a soft pencil; allow approximately 2 mm ($\frac{1}{16}$ in) oversize for subsequent trimming. Lay the straight edge to the marked line and hold steady whilst lightly scoring the laminate surface with the cutter, *see Fig. 1*. Having established a groove in the surface, make two or three more passes using slightly more pressure to cut well into the laminate backing. Still holding the straightedge in position, lift the free side of the laminate upward until it snaps off, *see Fig. 2*. Curved cuts can be made with the scoring tool by joining a series of small straight cuts. Alternatively a scissor type cutter **H** may be used.

Bonding

A contact adhesive, that is an adhesive which bonds immediately upon contact, without sustained pressure, is the normal method of fixing. Most types of contact adhesive allow no margin for error as a firm joint is made immediately, but some makes allow a limited amount of adjustment after contact.

A serrated spatula **B** is normally used for spreading.

Alignment

Most adhesives form a solid bond immediately contact takes place; therefore it is vital that pre-contact alignment be accurate. A simple method here is to lay thin strips of timber or hardboard between the coated surfaces so that the laminate may be accurately adjusted before contact. The strips are then progressively removed as contact is made, *see Fig. 3*.

Trimming

After bonding, the laminate overhang must be trimmed flush to the backing material.

An ideal tool for this work is the plane **F** which uses easily replaceable pre-sharpened blades. Overhang to short or shaped edges may be trimmed using a medium file **D**.

Edge trim

Purpose made flexible edge trim is available in rolls **G** and being much thinner than the main sheet material, may be cut using stout scissors **E**. This type of trim is best applied after the main sheet covering. After cutting to length the trim and backing surface are adhesive-coated and then left for the normal drying period. The trim can then be pressed firmly into position with equal overhang to both sides. A medium file **D**, angled slightly away from the main surface, is suitable for trimming away the overhang.

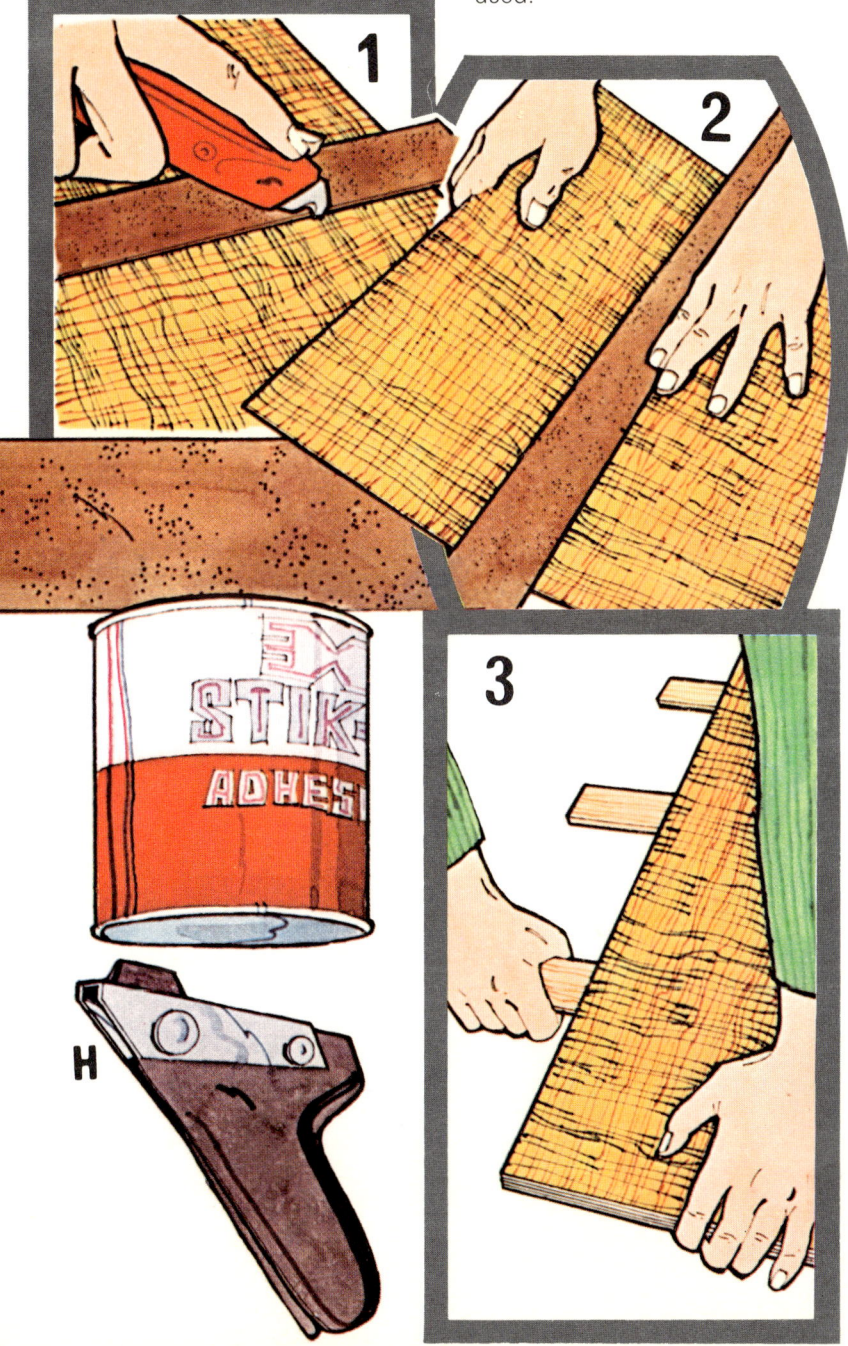

Room Divider/ Storage System

This versatile system is built up from a series of easily constructed boxes which are then arranged to form a desired layout for a room divider, as pictured, or to provide wall storage units for living room, study or office. Each part of the unit, being completely independent, means that re-arrangement is simply a matter of arranging the boxes to suit a location or desired effect. The unit shown, *fig. 1,* consists of four boxes, although of course these could be more, or less, as required.

Whilst general dimensions of the boxes are not critical it is important that their sizes of all parts match up in one direction. For instance, all the boxes shown measure 355mm (14") along at least one side. This means that the scope of possible layouts is wide because the boxes will present a level building platform, and even allow bridging between two parts. Combinations and layouts are virtually limitless and in addition to the styles pictured and mentioned, the boxes can be used to build a desk, a coffee table, a Hi-Fi and record housing unit.

To keep construction simple the units have been designed around plastic laminate, which is used not only to provide an elegant and durable finish, but also to cover the simple screwed butt joint construction. The work is straightforward but it is important that the sequence of laminate covering and assembly be strictly followed.

The sliding door arrangement is added as required, after main construction, by bonding a plastic sliding door channel to the inner edge of both sides of the unit. The doors are made up from two thicknesses of laminate, bonded back to back.

CUTTING LIST FOR FIG. 1 OPPOSITE
Tools Required
Set square, measure, drill, 50 mm (2") No. 8 screw combination bit, plane, file, panel saw, laminate cutting tool, medium screwdriver, pin hammer.

Plastic Laminate (All Units)
For inside facings take sizes from cutting list right, allowing 2 mm ($\frac{1}{16}$") oversize all round for trimming. For outer covering take sizes direct from assembled structure, allowing 2mm ($\frac{1}{16}$") all round for trimming.
50 mm (2") No. 8 countersunk steel woodscrews (approximately 60 for unit shown)
38 mm (1$\frac{1}{2}$") panel pins
Wood glue
Contact Adhesive
Edge trim (approximately 20 M (60') for unit shown).

No.	Length	Width	Material		Location
Large Unit					
2	1220 mm (48")	254 mm (10")	18 mm ($\frac{3}{4}$") Chipboard		Top & Bottom
2	317 mm (12$\frac{1}{2}$")	254 mm (10")	,,	,,	Ends
1	317 mm (12$\frac{1}{2}$")	228 mm (9")	,,	,,	Centre member
Cupboard Unit					
2	610 mm (24")	254 mm (10")	,,	,,	Top & Bottom
2	317 mm (12$\frac{1}{2}$")	254 mm (10")	,,	,,	Ends
Square Unit					
2	317 mm (12$\frac{1}{2}$")	254 mm (10")	,,	,,	Ends
2	355 mm (14")	254 mm (10")	,,	,,	Top & Bottom
Plinth Units (each)					
2	292 mm (11$\frac{1}{2}$")	100 mm (4")	,,	,,	Front & Back
2	215 mm (8$\frac{1}{2}$")	100 mm (4")	,,	,,	Sides

fig 1

Unit Construction

1 Mark out the various parts and cut to size.

2 Plane edges where necessary to ensure that all panels are square and accurate.

3 Cut laminate panels as the cutting list and bond to cover one complete face of all parts. Trim all edges square.

4 Fix top and bottom panels to the end panels, using simple butt joints glued and pinned, making certain that the laminate covered face is to the inside on all parts. Next use the combination screw drill bit to drill for three screws per joint, fit and tighten the screws. Trim all panels square and level with the plane and file; also check that all screw and nail heads are flush, not protruding.

5 Take the measurement for the external laminate covering direct from the assembled members. Cut panels to size and then bond to two opposing sides, trim all round and then add the remaining two sides. Carefully trim all round.

6 All edges are covered with 25 mm (1 in) wide edge trim to match the main covering material. For a neat appearance all edge trim corners should be mitre joined. Use the file to cut the edge trim nearly to the main covering. Finish by rubbing all sharp edges lightly with fine glass paper wrapped around a timber block.

7 Plinth units are made by glueing and screwing the front and back members to the end members (see cutting list). External faces are then covered with laminate.

8 Sliding doors may be fitted using a plastic sliding door track bonded around the inner edge of the unit. Doors are made up by bonding two thicknesses of laminate back to back; take door sizes direct from structure after fitting the plastic track.

Internal Wall and Ceiling Preparation

All furniture and floor coverings must be removed from the room or adequately protected before work is started.

For simple preparation the following tools will be required.

A. A dust sheet to protect the floor.

B. A plastic bucket and sponge for soaking old wallpaper and washing down walls.

The key to a successful decorating job lies in careful surface repair and preparation. This applies whether the work is being carried out in or outdoors, to plaster, brick, wood or metalwork, as even the best quality finishing materials will give less than best if applied to a poor surface.

Almost as important as preparation is planning. Here a preliminary survey should be carried out and careful note made of various jobs involved, together with a list of tools and materials. The notes can be used to prepare a simple schedule of work, the layout of which will vary from job to job. Generally, however, alterations and heavy repair work should be listed first, followed by making good, washing down etc., and to final decoration. The schedule can save much time and frustration by helping to steer an organised course through all stages of the job, particularly important for the novice decorator or where two or more helpers are involved. Gathering the tools and materials listed, before work starts, will minimise unnecessary hold-ups and again help the work run smoothly.

C. A wire brush, necessary where some types of plastic-coated wallpaper have to be stripped.

D. A non-flexible scraper.

E. A square piece of hardboard or plywood as a pallette for plaster filler.

F. A flexible bladed filling knife.

G. Plaster filler.

H. A cork sanding block and fine sandpaper.

J. A hand brush for general dusting down.

A pair of steps will also be required.

Ceiling

The standard finish for ceilings is emulsion paint and this should be washed with a weak detergent mix and rinsed. Any loose finishes or flaking areas should be scraped back to solid material.

Walls

Previously emulsion painted walls should be washed and rinsed as described. Standard wallpaper should be well soaked with either warm detergent or diluted wallpaper stripper, and then the paper stripped away as *Fig. 1*. With plastic coated wallpaper a wire brush must be scrubbed over the surface, *Fig. 2*, in order to allow water to penetrate for subsequent stripping as *Fig. 1*. Where ready pasted paper is to be stripped, then this does not require initial soaking. Having released one corner, the complete facing may be pulled away, leaving the backing, which may then be soaked and scraped away. After all paper has been removed the walls should be washed and rinsed.

Minor Cracks

Minor cracks should be filled using a plaster type filler and a flexible bladed filling knife, *Fig. 3*, and the whole wall surface lightly rubbed with fine sandpaper, *Fig. 4*.

Preparing Internal Woodwork

The general tools required for preparing previously painted indoor woodwork are:

A. Wet-or-dry abrasive paper.
B. Cork sanding block.
C. Real or imitation wash leather.
D. Paint stripper.
E. Stiff bladed scraper.
F. Shaped and triangular shave hook scrapers.
G. Pallette, filler and flexible bladed filling knife.
H. Plastic bucket.

Where door fittings, shelves and other fitments are to be removed, then a suitable screwdriver will also be required.

First stage of the preparation work is to remove, where possible, any locks, catches or bolts from doors or other woodwork, *Fig. 1*. This is easier and preferable to painting around or over such fittings, which may become jammed or difficult to operate if clogged with paint.

Where the existing paintwork is sound, then preparation is simply a matter of rubbing away the old gloss finish in order to provide a 'key' for the new paint. A dust-free method of carrying this out is to use 'wet-or-dry' abrasive paper **A** dipped into a mild water/detergent mix and then wrapped around a cork sanding block **B**. The paper should be rinsed in the water from time to time to release old paint from the pores, and the rubbed paintwork wiped clean and dry with the leather **C**. This method of rubbing down provides a superior surface to the traditional dry sandpapering technique, and in addition creates less mess.

Where the existing paint surface is not sound then it must be completely removed in order to provide a firm base for the new paintwork.

A readily available means of removing the old paint is to use a liquid paint stripper **D**. This is normally applied direct to the old paint surface, using a cheap paint brush. After a few minutes the paint will begin to blister, *Fig. 2*, and is then ready for scraping away with a stiff bladed scraper **E**. For awkward corners either the shaped or triangular shave hook scraper **F** may be used as *Fig. 3*. Before using paint stripper always check carefully the manufacturers' instructions as to use and safety. Also check instructions for washing down the woodwork after use, as it is important to remove all traces of the stripper before new paint is applied.

Make good any defects in the woodwork using a wood filler, hardboard pallette and flexible bladed filling knife **G**. Finally rub down bare wood with medium sandpaper.

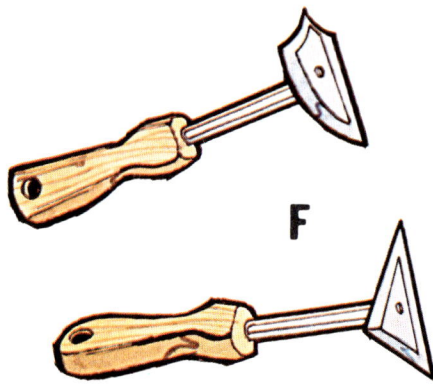

F

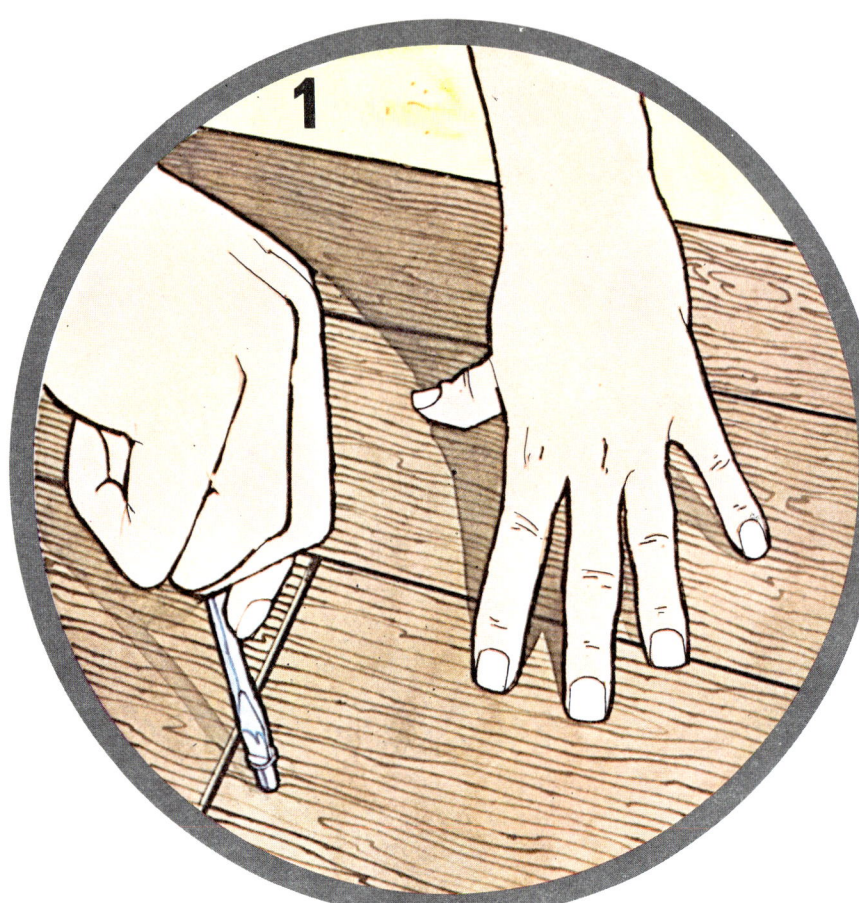

Repairs to Internal Woodwork

Where, in the initial survey, seriously defective woodwork has been found, then remedial action should be effected before the final stages of preparation are carried out.

Floorboards

The odd loose floorboard is a fairly common problem, and is often found where plumbing or electrical work has been carried out and a short length of board removed giving access to the floor void.

It may well be that water pipes or electricity cables run close under the loose board, so avoid the temptation to simply hammer nails in, as this may lead to serious damage and possibly danger of electric shock or fire. Remove the loose board to check underside clearance and then drill through in a clear space and refix, using countersunk wood screws, as *Fig. 1*. For short lengths of board this method is preferable to nailing, which will often split the wood. Subsequent removal is also simplified.

Should there be any evidence of condensation forming on the underside of the board, rotting or infestation with woodworm, then it is advisable to have the floor surveyed by a specialist before proceeding further.

Skirting Board

Where a fireplace or piece of fitted furniture has been removed a gap is often left in the skirting board. Bridging the gap with a piece of matching board is the best method of repair, as *Fig. 2*. Most timber yards carry lengths of standard shaped modern skirting board as stock. However, where the existing board is old or of non-standard shape, a cardboard template of the section may be made and a piece of timber shaped by hand with a suitable plane. Alternatively the work may be let out to a local saw mill.

In carrying out the repair work the ends of the existing board should be prised away from the wall sufficiently to allow a vertical angled saw cut to be made, *Fig. 2*. The ends can then be re-fixed and the bridging piece cut and trimmed to a good fit. The standard method of fixing skirting board is by nailing to the wall, but where the new length is short, well countersunk screws and wall plugs should be used to avoid the possibility of the wood splitting, as may occur with nailing.

A non-water based filler should be used over the screw-heads, the end joints filled, and the whole sanded smooth.

Door and Window Beading

Loose architrave beading around doors and window frames should be checked and tacked back as necessary, using panel pins, *Fig. 3*. Where the timber is badly damaged or split, then standard shaped replacement lengths are normally readily available from timber stockists. The mitre corner joint can be accurately cut where necessary, using a mitre guide, see page 46 (Woodworking Joints No. 23). Fixing pins should be punched and filled with wood filler.

Doors

The first point to check with jamming or ill-fitting doors, are the hinges for security and correct fitting, see pages 32–33 (Hinges and Catches). Where the door needs trimming, this may be carried out with a woodworking plane or rasp type plane or file. The file is particularly useful for trimming the underside of external doors, a frequent trouble spot, without the need to remove the door, *Fig. 4*. Any visible planed areas should be lightly sanded over.

Repairs to
Internal Walls

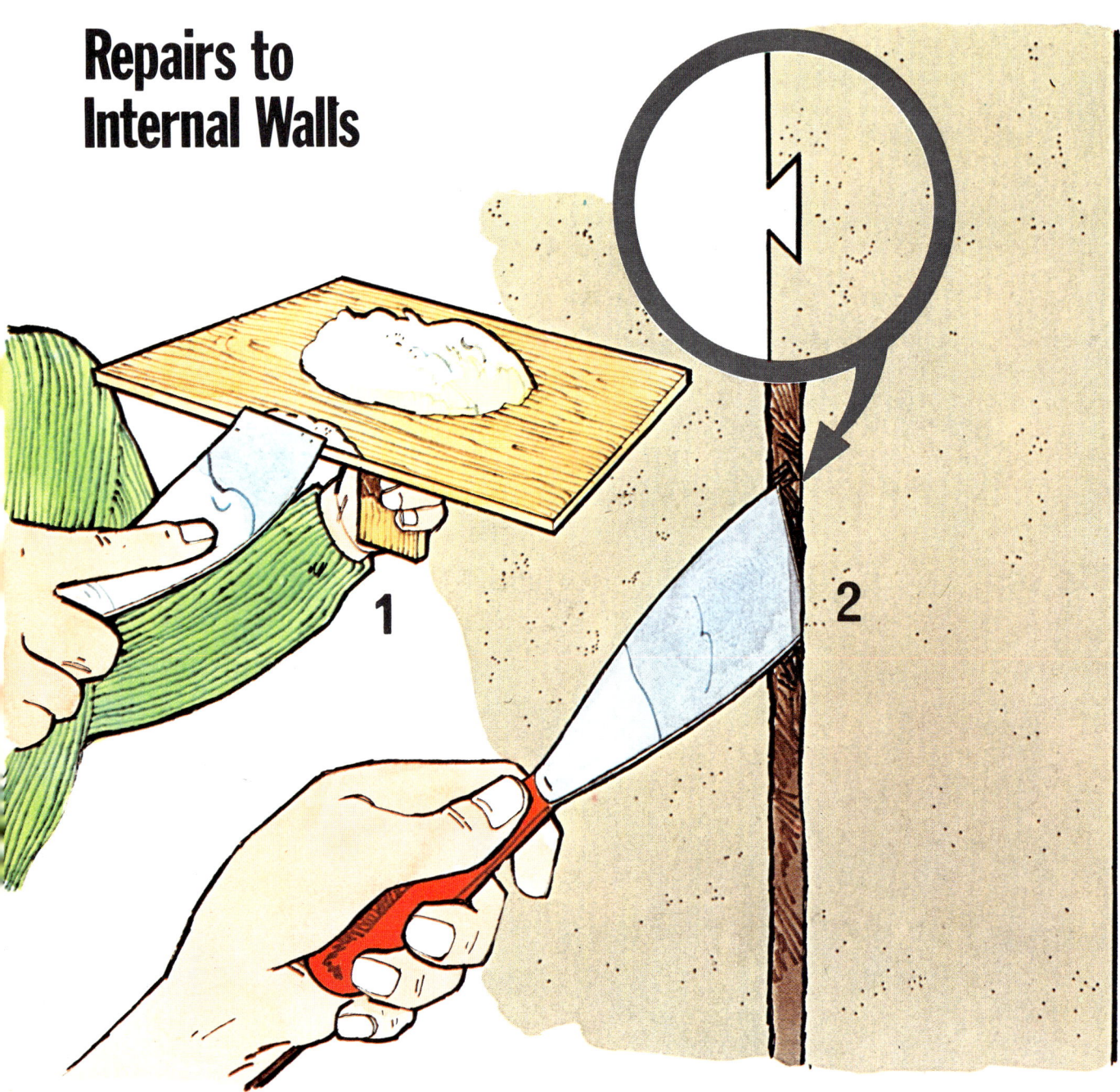

Repair work to walls and fixed wall finishes, other than minor cracks in plaster, should be carried out before final surface preparation.

Essential tools for filling work are shown in *Fig. 1* and consist of a square-edged and flat piece of hardboard or plywood to act as a hawk or pallette for the filler. The scraper or filling knife must be of the type with a highly polished and flexible blade. Filler should be picked up on the tip of the scraper blade and in small quantities only, the blade being frequently wiped clean as shown in *Fig. 1*, and recharged with filler during the course of the work.

Where large cracks are to be filled, it is as well to give the filler an additional 'key' by under-cutting the sides of the crack, as *Fig. 2*. This can be done with the edge of the scraper as illustrated, the object being to cut the base of the crack slightly wider than the surface hole. Any loose dust must be brushed out and then the filler pressed solidly home, using the flex in the scraper blade, to ensure complete penetration. With deep cracks, filler drying shrinkage will probably mean that a final skim over with filler will be necessary to produce a perfectly flush finish. This is preferable to overfilling and then sanding smooth.

Glazed Tiles

Replacing the odd damaged tile in a modern kitchen or bathroom

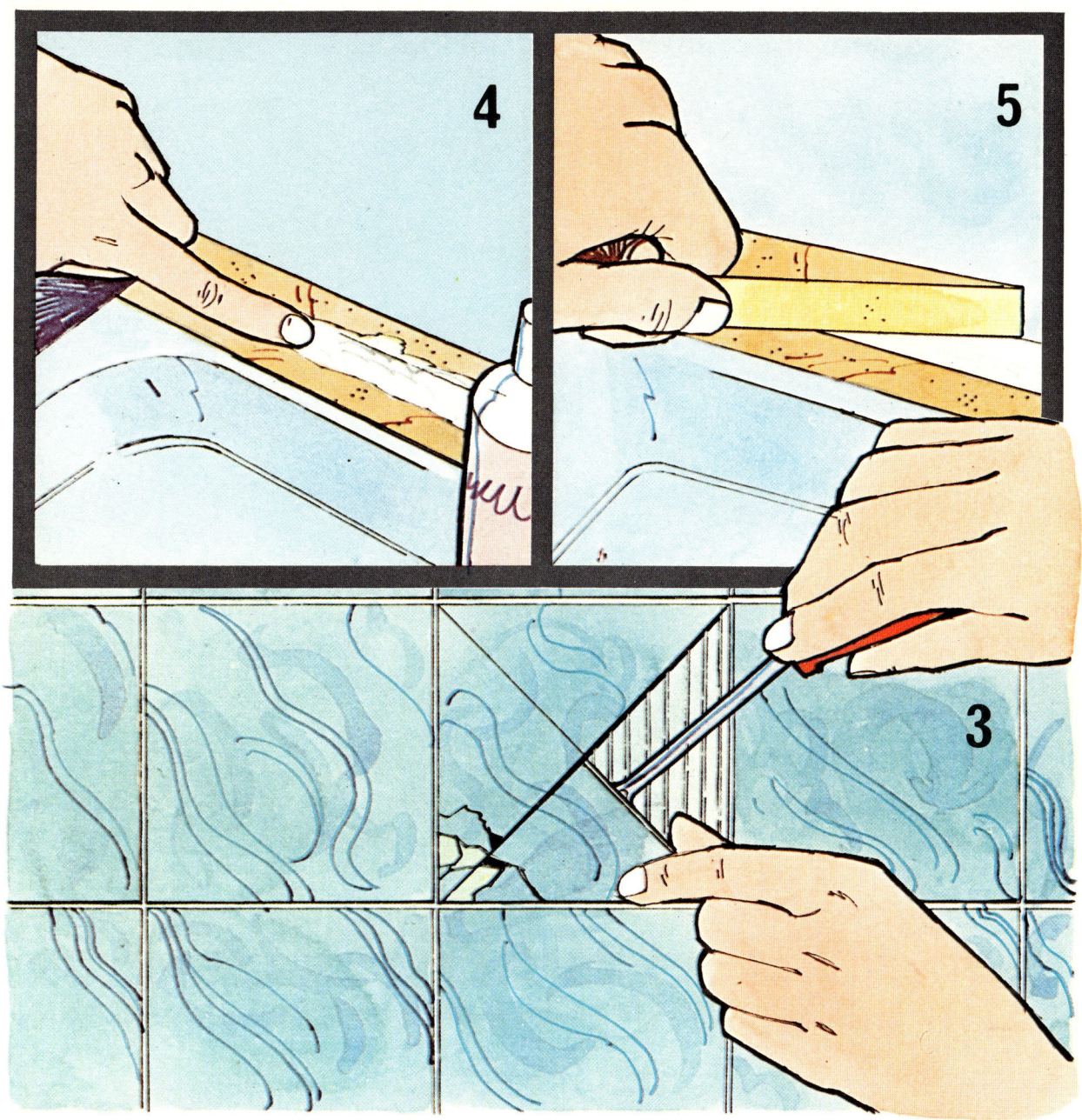

is a comparatively simple operation, the main problem being to avoid damaging surrounding good tiles.

The tile is first cut from corner to corner, in the form of an X, *Fig. 3*, using a glass or tile cutter. Tapping the centre will then cause it to split into four separate triangular pieces, which should be simple to prise away with an old screwdriver. After the old adhesive has been scraped away, a new tile can be fixed with tile adhesive and the joints re-grouted. The older type of large, heavy glazed tiles were often fixed to a strong, cement backing and whilst the method described will assist with removal, the work is much more difficult and will probably entail the use of a hammer and cold chisel to chip away the pieces of cut tile.

Cracks Around Sinks and Baths

For sealing the inevitable gap between sink or bath and adjoining tiled wall surface, a flexible, purpose-made sealer should be used. For a neat finish, strips of self-adhesive masking tape should be applied about 6 mm ($\frac{1}{4}$ in) either side of the gap. The sealant can then be squeezed into position direct from the tube, ironed smooth with a damp finger tip, *Fig. 4*, and then the tape pulled away, *Fig. 5*, to leave a straight and neat edge.

Painting Walls and Ceilings

Paint may be applied to walls and ceilings using:

A. Paint pads.
B. A paint roller.
C. Conventional paint brushes.

Where a roller or pads are to be used, then a purpose-made tray **D** for paint pads or **E** for a paint roller will also be required.

Much tray cleaning can be avoided if aluminium foil is used as a lining. Before using any paint the manufacturers' instructions as to surface preparation, primers, and recommended methods of application should be checked.

Paint Pads

Paint pads are used as *Fig. 1*, only the hair facing being dipped into the half filled tray, surplus paint being scraped lightly away against the inside edge of the tray. Application is as *Fig. 2*, the pad being pressed to the wall and moved steadily sideways.

Paint Roller

The paint roller presents a simple method of covering a large area of wall quickly. In use the tray should be filled with paint about half-way up the sloping bottom. The roller can then be charged by running backwards and forwards into the edge of the paint, as *Fig. 3*. Charging should continue until the roller is evenly impregnated with paint. Application is as *Fig. 4* and in random strokes. A 50 mm (2 in) conventional paint brush must be used in conjunction with the roller to cut in around doors and window frames and to fill in

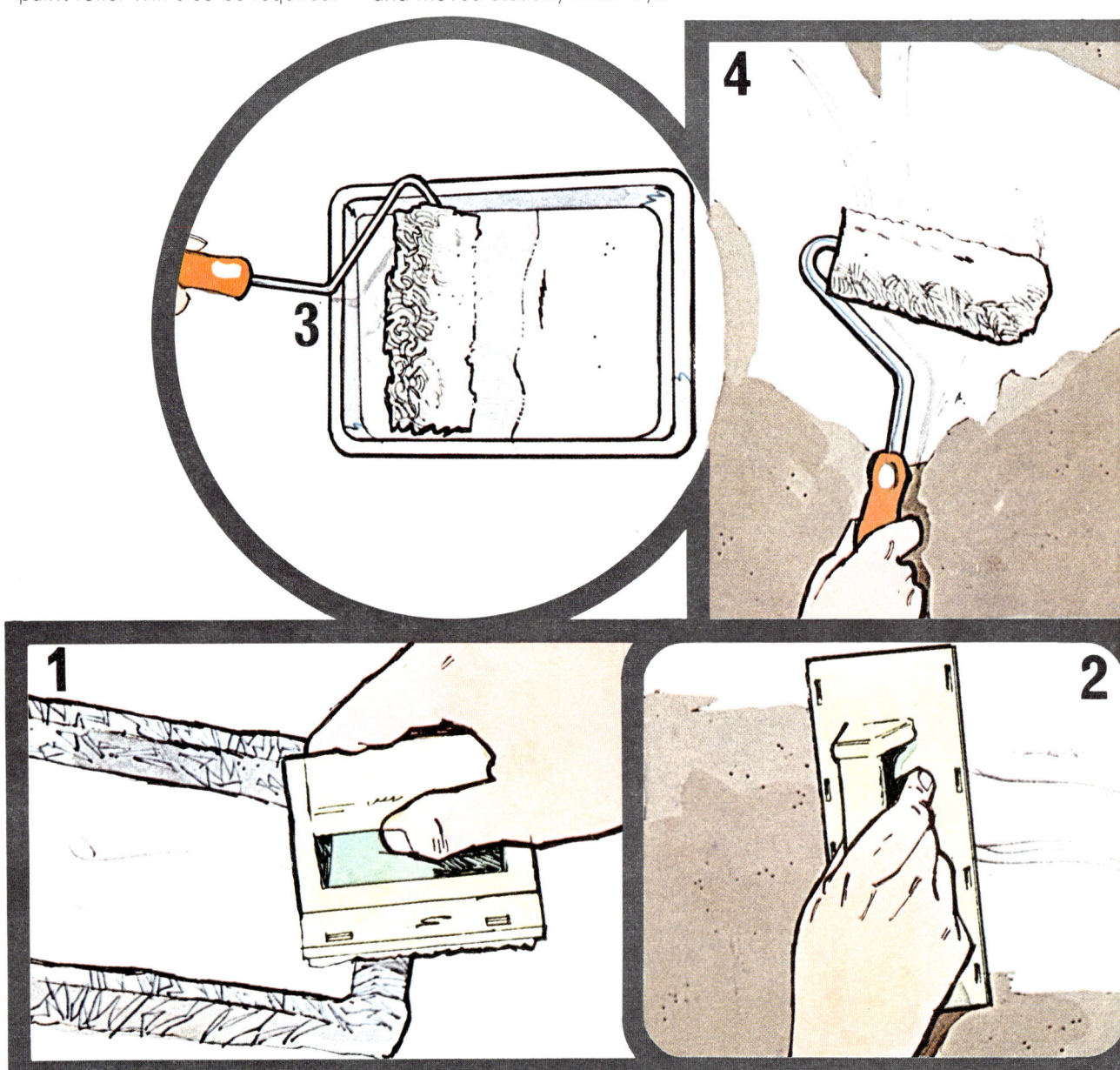

awkward edges and corners. Filling in is best done as work proceeds and before the roller is applied.

Paint Brushes

A 150 mm (6 in) conventional brush is suitable for painting the main areas of walls and ceilings, but a 50 mm (2 in) brush will also be required for cutting in and filling awkward corners, as with the roller. When charging the brush with paint, only half the bristle depth should be dipped in and care taken to see that the brush is not over-loaded, manufacturers' instructions on this point being carefully followed. A comfortable method of holding the brush is illustrated in *Fig. 5* and the degree of brushing out, after application, must again be governed by the manufacturers' instructions.

Painting Internal Woodwork

The secret of obtaining a really superb surface to finished paintwork lies in careful preparation and absolute cleanliness of work, tools and paint. Not only does careful painting show up in appearance of the final result, but the general 'life' of the work is also considerably extended. A smooth finish is easier to clean and far less likely to become grimy through impregnation of dust and dirt.

Essential tools to achieve a good finish are good quality brushes or paint pads. For the standard indoor woodwork,

the top of the paint kettle, *Fig. 1*, presents a simple method of carrying this out. The paint should be well stirred before straining.

Application

The number of coats of paint necessary to obtain a good finish depends on the existing surface. *Fig. 2* illustrates the various stages of painting bare timbers to a good quality gloss finish.

Initially, **A** the timber must be sanded smooth with all imperfections filled with a wood filler. Any knots must then be treated with a purpose made liquid knotting preparation to prevent any resin in the wood 'bleeding' through the paint.

Subsequent stages consist of **B** a coat of primer, followed by two undercoats, **C** and **D**, to build up a solid and firm colour base for the final top coat, **E** Each coat must be left to harden thoroughly before the next is applied and each coat should be lightly rubbed down with fine abrasive paper. To ensure absolute cleanliness and to avoid the possibility of dust or hair spoiling the work, a vacuum cleaner should be used to clean up at each stage.

Where a matt, or semi-matt, finish is required then the same paint can often be used for all three coats **C D** and **E**. With all types of paint the manufacturers' instructions in respect of stirring, thinning, undercoats, application, etc., should always be carefully followed.

Where a previously painted surface is to be repainted, then generally, where the colour change is not drastic, one undercoat followed by one top coat will provide a good finish.

Masking Tape

Masking tape **F**, applied around windows, *Fig. 3*, not only provides a clean and straight edge to the paintwork, but also ensures a full coat to the edge of the work.

three sizes of brush will normally suffice:
A. A 15 mm ($\frac{1}{2}$ in) for small window or door beading.
B. A 25 mm (1 in) for window and similar frames.
C. A 50 mm (2 in) for doors and larger areas.

With paint pads **D** a 25 mm (1 in) and 75 mm (3 in) should be suitable for general work. Where a number of flush doors are to be painted, then a short haired paint roller can be usefully employed (see page 64). Other useful items are **E** a paint

kettle, simply a metal can with rounded top edges and fitted with a wire handle to use as a dispenser for the paint, and **F** a roll of purpose made, self adhesive paint masking tape.

A skin will often form on the surface of paint stored in a part-used can, and this must be removed before re-use. The main area of skin can generally be lifted away, using an old screwdriver or stick, but odd particles left in the paint can only be removed by straining. A discarded nylon stocking tied across

Hanging Wallcovering 1

Wallpapering is best carried out after ceiling painting or papering, and after all woodwork painting is complete. Basic tools are:

A. Purpose made pasting table or other flat surface on which to lay paper for pasting and cutting.

B. 150 mm (6 in) brush for pasting.

C. Plastic bucket to contain mixed paste and with a length of string tied across the handle fixings as a brush rest.

Items A, B and C are not essential where a ready-pasted paper is to be used. Here item **D**, a tray type water container in which to dip the paper, is required.

E. Sponge for smoothing ready-pasted paper.

F. Brush for smoothing pasted paper.

G. Soft pencil for general marking work.

H. Steel tape rule.

J. Plumb bob for establishing and marking verticals.

K. Wallpaper scissors for general trimming work.

L. Knife, useful for trimming vinyl and heavier type papers.

M. Seam roller for running over butt joints to ensure a flat surface.

N. Straightedge rule for measuring and marking, and also useful as an edge against which to steady the knife L.

A safe working platform will be required; also a bucket of clean water and swab.

Estimating

Wallcoverings are generally sold in rolls 10·5 metres (11 yds) long × 520 mm (20½ in) wide. To calculate the approximate number required: **A.** Measure ceiling height and divide into roll length. **B.** Measure around

the walls and divide by roll width. Divide **A** by **B** to arrive at the approximate number of rolls. Large doors and windows will reduce the number required. A large or complicated wallcovering pattern may increase the number.

As with most jobs, successful wallpapering depends to a great extent on individual patience, skill and experience. Wallcoverings are available in a range of materials from the standard paper types to the modern, readypasted vinyls. To ensure best results, careful attention must always be paid to manufacturers'

recommendations and instructions, especially in respect of suitable adhesives.

Where wall covering is to be applied to new or porous plaster then a 'sizing' coat will be required. Generally a standard paste as used for the covering is suitable. This should be diluted according to the manufacturers' instructions and brushed freely onto the plaster surface.

Getting Started
The first length of covering should be cut, sufficiently oversize to allow for trimming, and

then used as a pattern for subsequent full length cutting. Before further lengths are cut, however, it is important that the horizontal pattern match be carefully checked. Cut lengths are laid, face down, on the pasting table.

Hanging should proceed away from the lightest part of the room, normally a window, and work toward the main door. To ensure that the covering is hung truly vertical, a line must be established on the wall against which the first length of paper is hung. This is achieved by using a rule to mark the width of the paper from the starting point, Fig. 1. The plumb line is then coated with chalk (or plaster filler) and hung from the pencil mark, using a drawing pin or adhesive tape for a fixing. The chalked line is then 'snapped' with the fingers, as Fig. 2, to produce an accurate vertical line on the wall.

Pasting is carried out as Fig. 3, working from the bottom of the pattern, the covering being folded concertina fashion, pasted face to pasted face, as work proceeds.

Hanging Wallcovering 2

Where a heavy paper is used the paste must be given time to soak in so that the paper will swell and become more supple. Subsequent hanging is then simplified, with minimal risk of air bubbles forming.

The first length of pasted and folded paper should be removed from the pasting table and laid on a clean surface. The second, and possibly the third, lengths, depending on the weight of the paper, may then be pasted and subsequent work arranged so that some paper is pasted, soaked and ready to use at all times. Experience with the first length or two will quickly establish a pattern.

Picking up a length of pasted and folded paper from the 'top' (the last end to be pasted) should allow the folds to drop away, leaving approximately one metre of paper still folded at the 'bottom'. The length is then positioned on the wall against the vertical line previously established. After the top half is accurately aligned, the bottom fold can be pulled away and the paper flattened to the wall with a brush, *Fig. 1*.

With a ready-pasted paper, the cut length is immersed in the water filled tray and then pulled out, as *Fig. 2*, hung immediately, and then sponged off, as *Fig. 3*.

With many complicated and floral patterned coverings, it is as well to pattern check at this stage, as *Fig. 4*, with the second length. Often it is only by seeing two adjoining pieces that the complete pattern run can be followed and any mistake with the first length would, at this point, be simple to rectify.

Trimming

With most coverings the standard wallpaper scissors can be used for top and bottom trimming, but first the surface of the covering should be carefully smoothed, as *Fig. 1 and 3*, to ensure that no trapped air bubbles remain. With most standard weight papers the back of the scissors can be used as a convenient means of creasing the paper along the trim mark. *Fig. 5* illustrates the method where the scissors are run over the paper and along the top of the skirting board to form a neat and accurate cutting mark. The paper is then pulled away from the wall and the scissors used to cut along the crease, *Fig. 6*; the trimmed paper should then flap neatly back into position. To ensure that no air bubbles remain, the area must be smoothed over. First, however, it is advisable to wipe away any excess paste that may have been transferred to the skirting board, using a clean swab. This will prevent the smoothing brush or sponge becoming contaminated with paste.

Trimming between ceiling and wall can be carried out in a similar manner, but extra care must be taken to avoid excess paste being transferred to the finished ceiling surface. Holding the top edge of the paper away from the ceiling, whilst scissor marking is in progress, assists here, but where a thin paper is being used care must be taken to avoid tearing.

An important point to consider when trimming is disposal of waste pieces. Under no circumstances should they be dropped on the floor, as being paste-coated the surface is slippery and this presents a danger to people in the room. As each piece is cut away it should be folded, paste side to paste side, and deposited in a waste bin or sack.

With the first piece hung and trimmed, subsequent full length hanging is continued in a similar manner, the pattern being carefully edge matched, as *Fig. 4*, to a neat butt joint edge.

Hanging Wallcovering 3

As hanging and trimming progresses, butt joints can be neatly flattened to a uniform surface, using a simple seam roller tool, *Fig. 1*.

With some types of coverings, vinyls and heavyweights for instance, trimming is often easier using a knife as *Fig. 2*.

Trimming Around Doors and Windows

Generally where a window or door is encountered, only part of the covering length will overlap and need trimming. *Fig. 3* illustrates the first step where an initial horizontal cut is made and then the lower flap flattened to the wall as *Fig. 4*. The internal

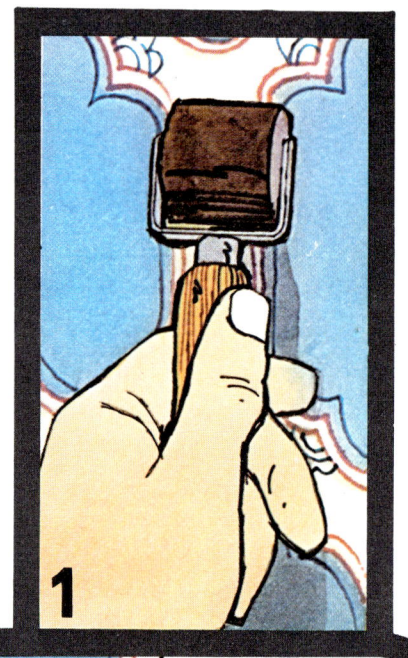

1

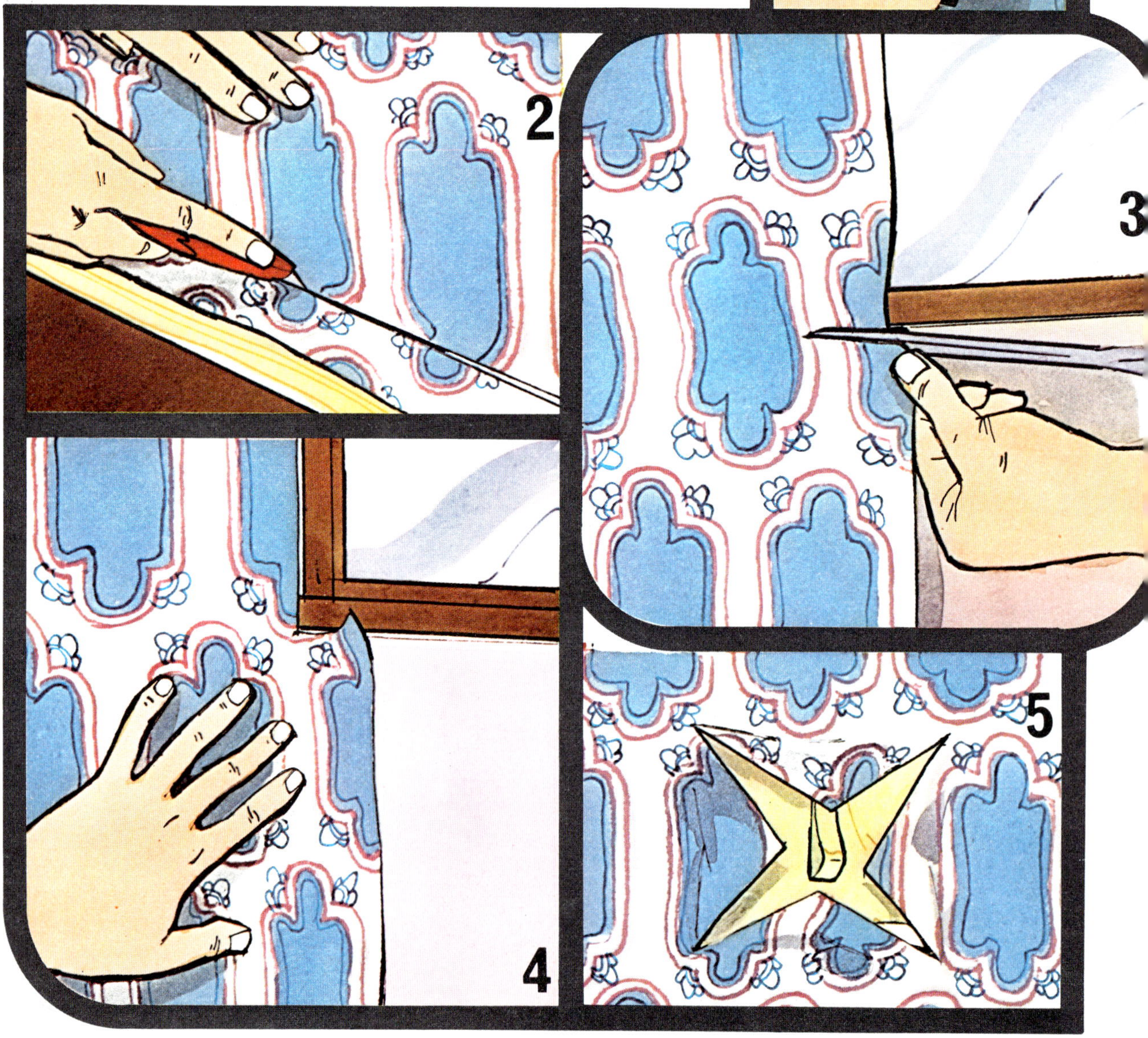

2

3

4

5

corners, *Fig. 5.* After the covering has been neatly pressed around the switch, final trimming can be either by scissors or knife.

Ceilings
A vital point here is a safe, full length working platform. An accurate start line is first established by the line-snapping method, see page 69, with the chalk coated line securely fixed at both ends with drawing pins. The line is snapped, the paper width less a 15 mm ($\frac{1}{2}$ in) corner overhang, from the wall. The pasted and folded covering is then laid across a rolled length of covering as a convenient means of horizontal manoeuvring, *see Fig. 6*, and, after initial positioning against the chalked line, unfolded and flattened.

angle of the overlapping piece is then marked and cut with scissors or knife. Negotiating the far side of the frame is generally best carried out by sticking the first full length piece lightly in position at the top and then carefully matching up the underframe pattern before making the initial horizontal cut, as *Fig. 3.* Where the main strip is less than about 150 mm (6 in) it may well prove easier to carry the horizontal cut completely across, align the lower piece, and then butt join the matching cut edges.

Negotiating Corners
Corners of plastered walls are rarely sufficiently square to allow any appreciable width of covering to be neatly wrapped around. With internal corners a strip is cut and hung to allow an approximate 15 mm ($\frac{1}{2}$ in) corner overlap. The remaining half of the cut length should then butt join to the overhang. However, where a neat butt join is not possible, the covering may be overlapped and a knife and straightedge used to cut vertically through the centre of the overlap. Pulling away the off-

cuts should leave a neat and accurate joining cut to both pieces.

With external corners a similar procedure as outlined is generally best to adopt, but the overhang flap size should be increased to about 50 mm (2 in).

Light Switches
Here the covering is pressed lightly in place over the switch and then cut with a knife or scissors from the centre to the

Lining Papers
Where a plastered surface is in poor general condition, or where certain types of textured papers are to be hung, a purpose-made lining paper is sometimes applied. The general hanging technique is as described, except that conflicting vertical butt joints can be avoided if the lining paper is applied in the opposite direction, generally horizontally, to the main covering, *Fig. 7.*

Exterior Decoration: Access

1

2

3

4

A vital aspect of house decorating and repair work is that of access, and a safe working platform suitable for the job in hand must always be a prime consideration.

Fig. 1 illustrates a portable tower-type scaffolding system, built up to desired height simply by slotting together pre-welded tubular frames. The system is suitable for most applications, from painting to building work.

Comparatively high initial cost, coupled with storage space requirements, tend to put the scaffolding tower outside the scope of the home handyman. However the equipment is generally available in many areas from tool hire concerns.

Fig. 2 illustrates a ladder

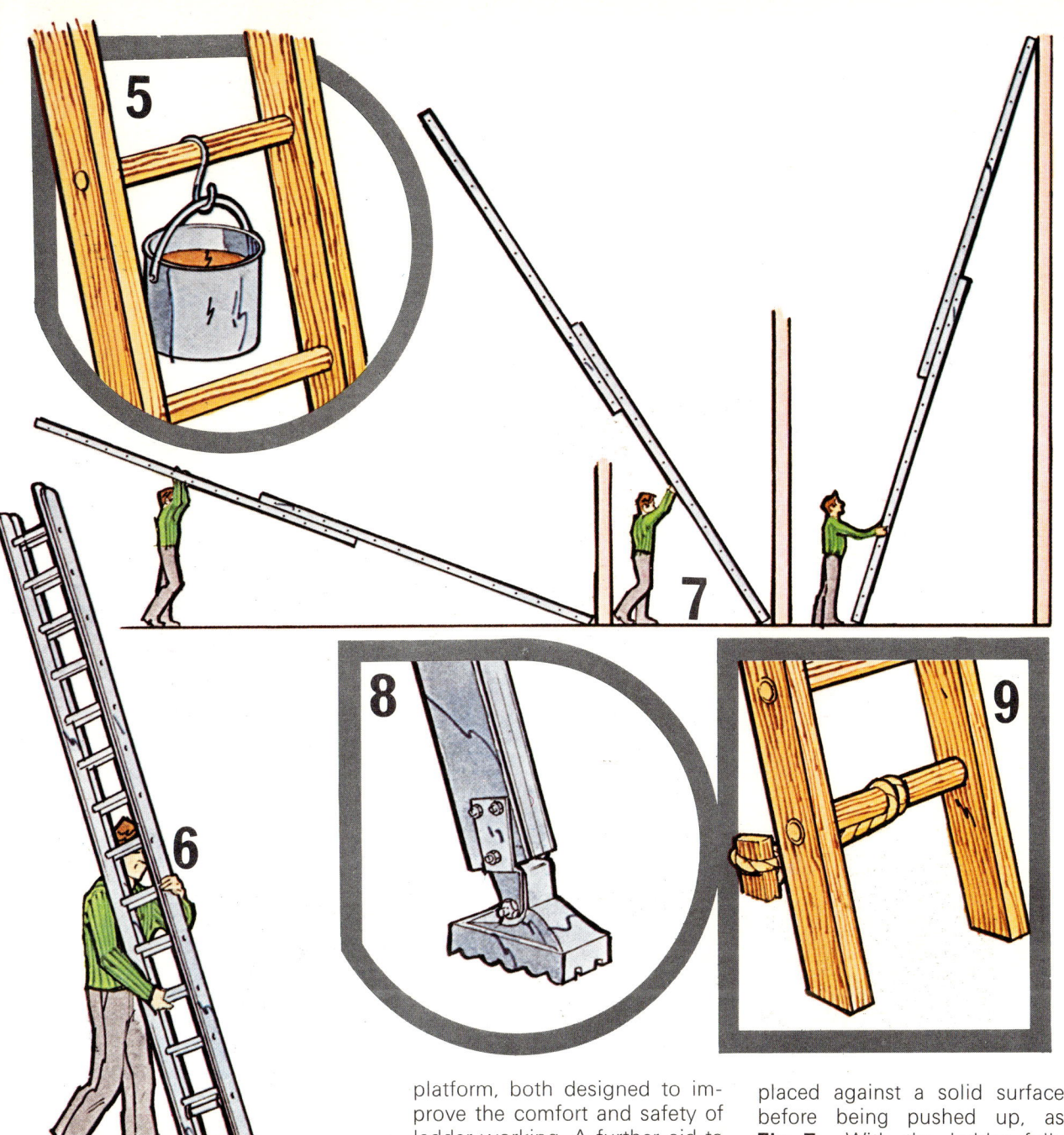

cripple, consisting of a portable metal frame, erected between two standard ladders to hold a working platform and safety rail. Ideal for painting and other light repair and maintenance work. Again this type of equipment is generally available from tool hire concerns.

Fig. 3 illustrates a ladder stand-off, and **Fig. 4** a ladder

platform, both designed to improve the comfort and safety of ladder working. A further aid to off-ladder working is illustrated in **Fig. 5** and consists simply of a metal 'S' hook, used to hang a paint kettle from the ladder rung.

Ladders, especially the larger extending type, must be correctly handled if injury and damage are to be avoided. The ladder should be picked up, as **Fig. 6**, and carefully balanced against the shoulder, before any forward movement is made. Before setting up, the ladder should be extended as required and then

placed against a solid surface before being pushed up, as **Fig. 7** With the ladder fully erect, the lower part is pulled away to a distance equal to about a quarter of the height.

Purpose-made self-aligning feet for the foot of the ladder, **Fig. 8**, provide a convenient method of ensuring that the erected ladder does not slip. An alternative method, where the ladder is to be used either on or near soft ground, is illustrated, **Fig. 9**, where a stout timber peg is driven in to the ground and the ladder securely tied to this with rope.

External Repairs and Maintenance: Woodwork

External woodwork to most homes consists of window and door frames, and a common repair problem involves weatherproofing. The most vulnerable part of any outdoor timber frame is the join between various parts and materials. The glass and timber of a window frame for instance, or where a door frame connects to surrounding brickwork. A gap at this point, where water penetrates, can quickly lead to timber rotting problems. With a timber clad building gaps or joins between timbers, for instance where horizontal cladding meets a vertical door or window frame member, all represent potential leakage areas.

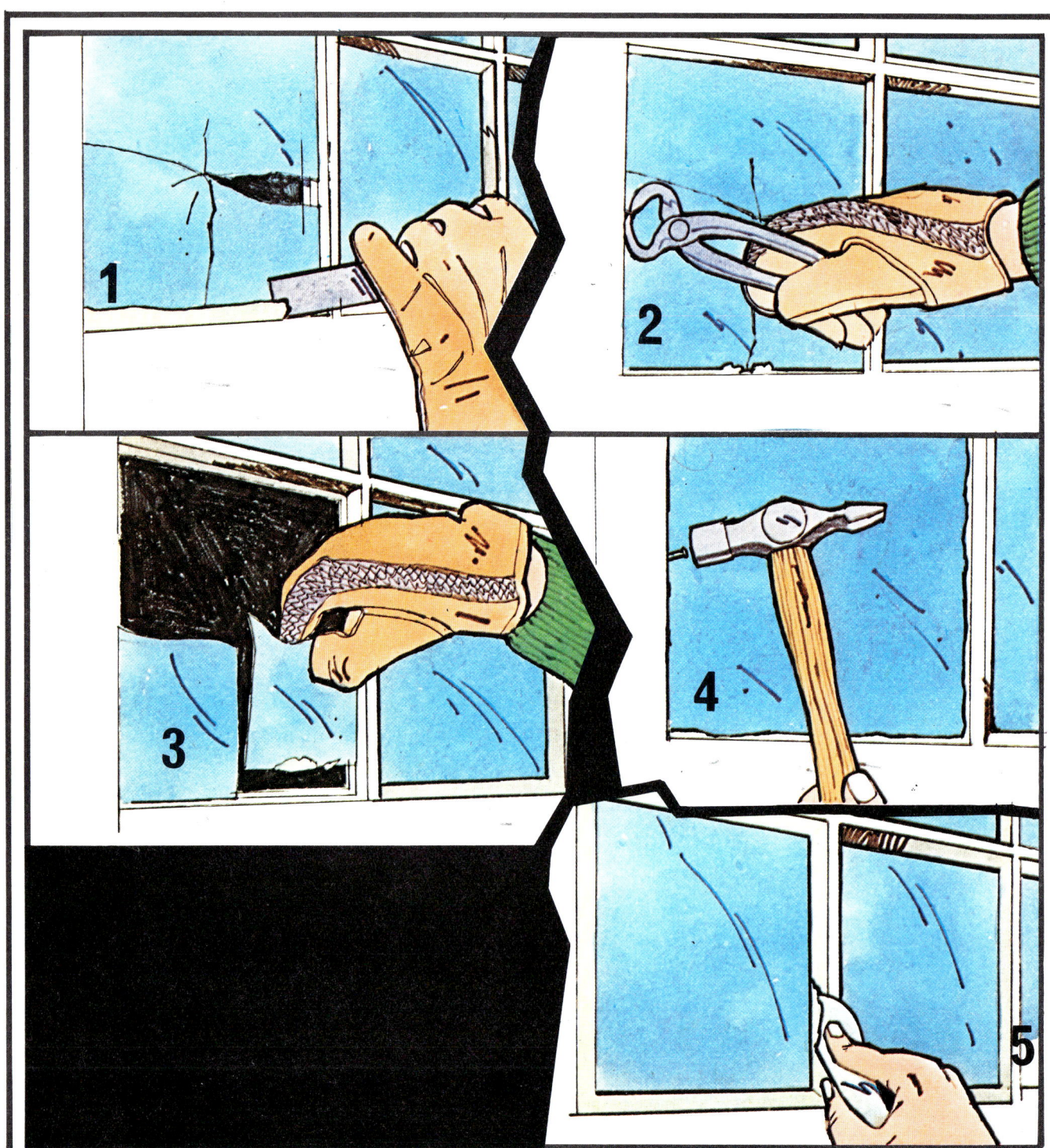

Windows

The standard method of sealing between the timber and glass of windows is with an oil-based putty.

To replace a broken or cracked window start by carefully measuring the frame size, i.e. to the outside edge of the existing putty joint. Reduce the measurement by about 2 mm ($\frac{1}{16}$ in) all round and order the replacement pane. Glass is available in a range of thicknesses and requirement here depends basically on window area, but also on exposure and usage. The supplier should be consulted on this point when ordering. Some putty and a few plated panel pins are also required.

Proceed as **Fig. 1**, wearing protective gloves, and dig out the existing putty with an old screwdriver or chisel. The window will probably be secured with some pins driven into the frame across the face of the glass; these are removed with a pair of pincers, **Fig. 2**, with care being taken to see that the broken glass does not accidentally fall away. After removal of the pins the broken glass can be lifted away as **Fig. 3**, the old putty seal under the glass must then be dug cleanly away, and replaced with some well kneaded new putty. The new pane is then pressed firmly into the putty and secured by some new pins, **Fig. 4**. The final putty seal must be pressed firmly home with the thumb before being trimmed flat with a putty knife, **Fig. 5**. The new putty should be left for about one week before painting over.

Frames

The standard method of sealing the inevitable gap between window and door frames and main building structure is by using a non-setting mastic material. This is generally available in convenient-to-use tubes fitted with an extended applicator nozzle. In use the nozzle of the tube is placed over the crack so that as the sealer is squeezed out it completely bridges the gap, leaving a neat convex shape. Although a skin eventually forms over the sealer, the main body of the material remains sufficiently flexible to maintain a seal.

External Repairs and Maintenance: Walls

The external masonry walls of a house must be kept in good order if serious deterioration and dampness penetration is to be avoided. In particular, all necessary repair work should be carried out before redecoration is started.

Brickwork

A common problem with brickwork, especially with older buildings, is that of deterioration of the mortar joint, or 'pointing' joint between bricks. The damage may be confined to small areas, possibly caused as a result of exposure to wind and weather or, where the original mortar mix was poor, to the whole building. In either case the procedure for repointing is the same and essential tools consist of a cold chisel and club hammer, used to remove the old mortar to a depth of about 15 mm ($\frac{1}{2}$ in), and a pointing trowel and mortar hawk as **Fig. 1**. A suitable mortar mix consists of one part cement and six parts sand, with either one part lime or a purpose-made liquid plasticiser added.

The mortar should be mixed in small quantities and used within one hour of mixing. Also the ingredients must be carefully measured to ensure a uniform colour to the finished work.

After the old mortar has been scraped clear, re-pointing is carried out as **Fig. 1**, with a strip of mortar being firmly pressed into the joint, the hawk being held directly below in order to catch any mortar droppings. A simple method of providing a neat convex finish to the new joint is to use an ironing tool, described on page 98. Alternatively the mortar can be trowel finished flush or weather angled.

Rubbing the wall surface over with a stiff hand brush, after the mortar has started to set, will improve the general appearance of the work.

Where the ground floor of the house is timbered, air ventilation bricks or registers will be included in the brickwork at low

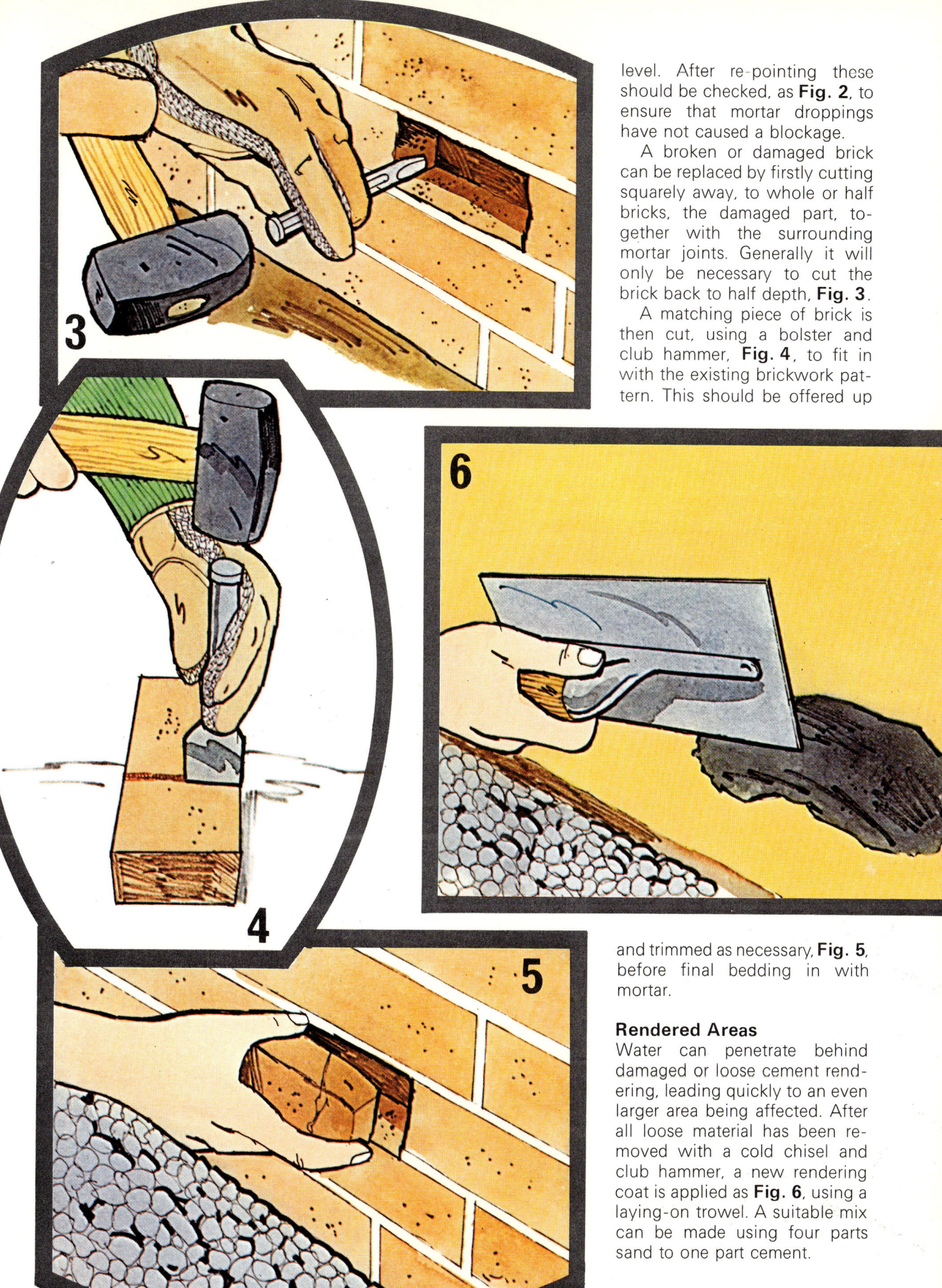

level. After re-pointing these should be checked, as **Fig. 2**, to ensure that mortar droppings have not caused a blockage.

A broken or damaged brick can be replaced by firstly cutting squarely away, to whole or half bricks, the damaged part, together with the surrounding mortar joints. Generally it will only be necessary to cut the brick back to half depth, **Fig. 3**.

A matching piece of brick is then cut, using a bolster and club hammer, **Fig. 4**, to fit in with the existing brickwork pattern. This should be offered up and trimmed as necessary, **Fig. 5**, before final bedding in with mortar.

Rendered Areas
Water can penetrate behind damaged or loose cement rendering, leading quickly to an even larger area being affected. After all loose material has been removed with a cold chisel and club hammer, a new rendering coat is applied as **Fig. 6**, using a laying-on trowel. A suitable mix can be made using four parts sand to one part cement.

Repairs and Maintenance: Roof and Gutter

The roof and rain gutter systems of a house, being constantly exposed to wind, rain and extremes of temperature, will quickly deteriorate if faults or breakages are neglected.

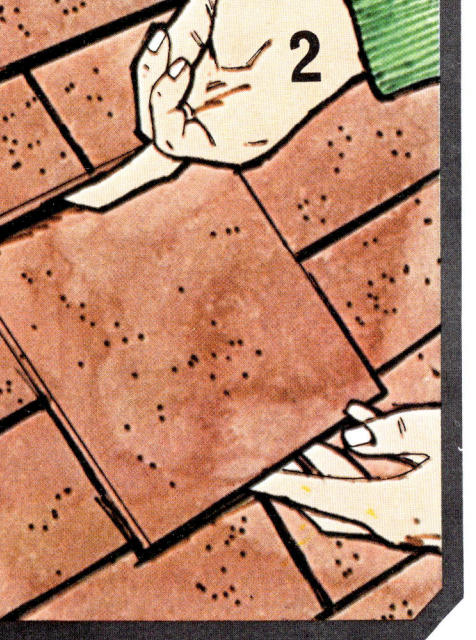

Roof Tiles

Most tiled roofing systems consist of concrete or clay tiles hooked over horizontally fixed timber tile battens by small lugs moulded to the underside of the tile, see page 104. Generally tile nailing is confined to random points and a broken tile can often be replaced simply by lifting the tiles immediately above and then pulling away the damaged tile. The replacement tile is then slipped under the lifted tiles, the lugs being eased over the tile batten. **Figs. 1** and **2** illustrate the process. Where a damaged tile is nailed, those immediately above can be slipped upward to expose the nail.

Flat Roof

The standard waterproofing for a flat roof consists of three layers of bitumen-bedded felt, see page 104, and where deterioration or a leak is found, purpose made compounds are available for simply brushing over, **Fig. 3**. However where the felt covering appears to be perished it may be necessary for the roof to be stripped and recovered.

Weather Flashings

Weather flashings are found where roofs butt to vertical walls; they are usually cut from lead sheet. Flashings to low pitched metal or plastic roofs are particularly susceptible to wind-driven rain penetration, if not carefully shaped to the corrugations. A piece of suitably sized wooden

dowelling can be used for this work, to shape the flashing as **Fig. 4**

Guttering

Modern rainwater disposal systems are made from plastic materials and, with many types, deterioration of the rubber gasket, **Fig. 5**, at junctions, end caps and other points, creates a leak. After renewal of the gasket, care must be taken that it is not displaced during re-assembly, **Fig. 6**. Joins in metal gutters are fixed with a nut and bolt and sealed with a metal type putty. Here the bolt will probably require cutting away with a hack saw before the joint can be dismantled. Old hardened putty must then be scraped away and the joint surfaces thoroughly dried before re-sealing with putty. A galvanised gutter bolt should be used for re-fixing.

Blockage by leaves or other debris is normally the cause of overflowing gutters and downpipes. The gutter can be quickly cleared using a piece of hardboard cut to the shape and used as a rake, **Fig. 7**. A blockage in the downpipe can sometimes be hooked out with a piece of stiff wire, or pumped through with a plunger, made up from a length of timber wrapped with rag, **Fig. 8**.

Preparing and Painting Woodwork

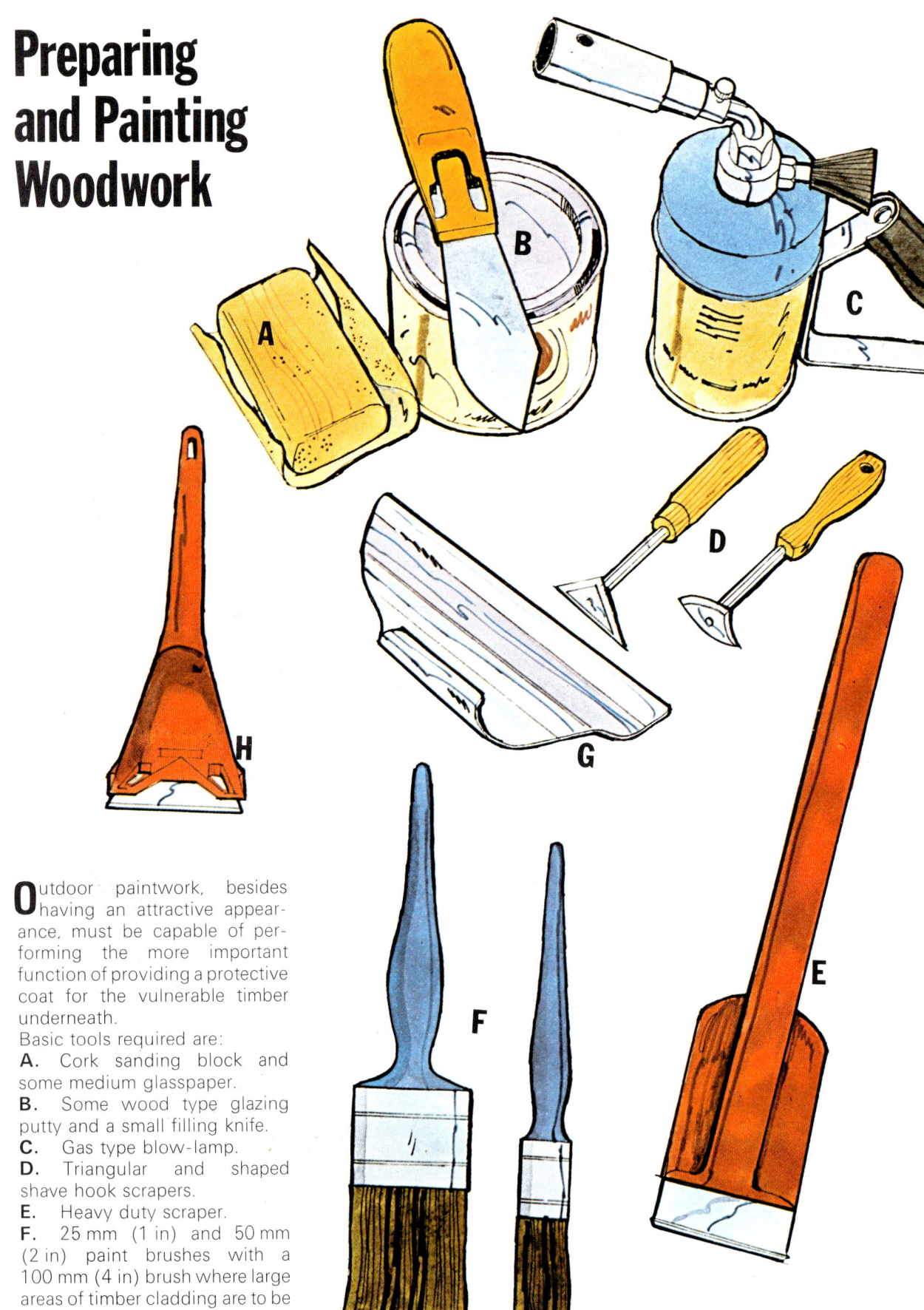

Outdoor paintwork, besides having an attractive appearance, must be capable of performing the more important function of providing a protective coat for the vulnerable timber underneath.

Basic tools required are:

A. Cork sanding block and some medium glasspaper.

B. Some wood type glazing putty and a small filling knife.

C. Gas type blow-lamp.

D. Triangular and shaped shave hook scrapers.

E. Heavy duty scraper.

F. 25 mm (1 in) and 50 mm (2 in) paint brushes with a 100 mm (4 in) brush where large areas of timber cladding are to be painted.

of sheet metal or other non-flammable material on the ground under the work area to catch scraped-away charred paint.

After all old paint has been scraped or burned away, the timber surface should be lightly glasspapered and all defects made good with wood filler or putty.

Repainting

The number of coats of paint necessary to obtain a durable finish depends on the type of paint used and the degree of preparation necessary. Subject to individual paint manufacturers' instructions, one undercoat followed by one top coat is generally sufficient where the original paintwork is sound. Where, however, bare timber is to be painted then a primer coat followed by two undercoats and one top coat will normally be required, see page 67.

A metal paint shield **G** provides a neat method of obtaining a straight paint line between glass and frame, *Fig. 2*. Where a shield of this type is not used, excess paint can be quickly scraped away using a replaceable-blade type scraper, **H**.

G. Aluminium paint shield.
H. Replaceable blade-type scraper.

Preparation

Where the existing paint coat is still firmly adhering to the woodwork, then preparation is mainly a matter of rubbing away the old gloss or dead paint surface, using glasspaper and block. Any dirt or grease present must be washed away with detergent and the surface rinsed and dried. Odd pieces of loose or damaged putty should be replaced after glass-papering. Putty can also be used to fill any nail holes and similar small defects in the woodwork.

Areas of dried-up and loose paint on flat surfaces can generally be quickly scraped away, using a heavy duty, replaceable-blade type scraper **E**. Where, however, the old paint is defective, extra thick or on shaped or narrow areas, a gas type blowlamp **C** can be used in conjunction with a shave hook **D** as a means of removal. In use, the tip of the flame of the blowlamp is used to heat up and soften the paint coat which is then immediately scraped away, *Fig. 1*. Extra care must be taken when using the blow-lamp not to scorch or burn the timber surface. The flame should be kept continually on the move and well away from any adjacent windows or inflammable material. It is advisable to lay a piece

Preparing and Painting Metalwork

The exterior metalwork of oil storage tanks, guttering, hinges and other fittings, will quickly rust through if the protective paintwork is allowed to deteriorate. The appearance of even small rust spots is a sure sign that attention is required and, if this cannot be effected immediately, then some first aid treatment in the form of a temporary paint coat over the rusting spot may well help to prevent excessive damage.

The basic tools are:
A. Electric drill, equipped with a cup type wire brush.
B. Protective eye goggles.
C. Hand-held wire brush.
D. 25 mm (1 in) or 50 mm (2 in) paintbrush, depending on the area to be painted.
E. Some chemical rust killer.
F. Glass reinforced plastic repair kit, useful where repair work has to be carried out.
G. Rasp type plane for filing smooth repaired glass fibre areas.

Preparation

As with all painting work, careful surface preparation is of the utmost importance if the new paint coat is to afford effective and lasting protection to the metal.

Where the paint surface is peeling and the metal surface rusty, then the electric drill-driven wire brush **A** should be used, as *Fig. 1*, to clean away the rust back to bright metal. Where the existing paint coat is sound, then any grease or dirt should be washed away with a rag dampened with white spirit, then brushed hard with either the hand brush **C** or drill-driven brush. During the course of both operations it is essential that protective eye goggles are worn.

Damage

Non-load bearing metal pipes or surfaces can be effectively repaired, using a glass fibre patch welded in position with a plastic resin filler. This material is generally available as a complete repair kit with full instructions. After wire brushing the damaged area, some mixed filler is applied followed by a suitably sized glass fibre patch. More filler is then pressed well into the patch, *Fig. 2*, and smoothed to shape.

After the filler has cured, it is planed to shape, using the rasp type plane **G**, *Fig. 3*.

Repainting

Before any paint is applied all previously rusted areas must be treated with a liquid rust killer applied to the manufacturers' instructions. This treatment is followed by a coat of metal primer, again over the bare areas only. Finally two full coats of paint, of a type recommended by the manufacturer for use with outdoor metal, should be applied.

Painting New Metal

Because the surface of metal is generally quite smooth, a special priming or 'etching' paint must be used before undercoats or finishing paints are applied. Basically two types of primer are available; a chromate which eats into the surface of the metal to obtain a firm grip, and a zinc or oxide type designed to provide a firm grip and base for the finishing coats. The type of primer to use depends on the make-up of the metal to be painted. Generally chromate primers are recommended for alloys, and zinc and oxide primers for ferrous metals. However the paint manufacturers' instructions should always be checked.

With new work, special care must be taken to ensure that any oil or grease is thoroughly cleaned away with white spirit before any primer or paint is applied.

Walls and Brickwork

There are two main reasons for painting external walls and brickwork. Firstly, purely for a decorative effect, and here many standard water-based emulsion paints are perfectly suitable. When paint is purchased for this purpose, the supplier should be informed of the intended use, and paint manufacturers' instructions and recommendations checked to see that a particular brand is suitable for outdoor application.

Another reason for painting walls is to afford protection against weather and frost penetration. Where, for instance, the surface of old brick facing is starting to crumble, purpose made outdoor wall finishes provide a reinforced and durable coating.

Tools Required

A. Paint roller, suitable for rapid application to reasonably smooth walls.

B. Soft hand brush for general dusting before painting.

C. Stiff bladed scraper for removing flaking paint and loose surface areas.

D. Flexible bladed scraper for applying filler to minor defects.

E. Purpose made outdoor plaster filler.

F. Stiff brush for brushing away loose surface material.

G. Purpose made wall painting brush, necessary for brick walls or other non-smooth surfaces.

Preparation

As with all painting work, appearance and durability of the final job depends on careful surface preparation and strict compliance with paint manufacturers' instructions concerning priming and application.

An essential for all types of paint is a firm and dust free base.

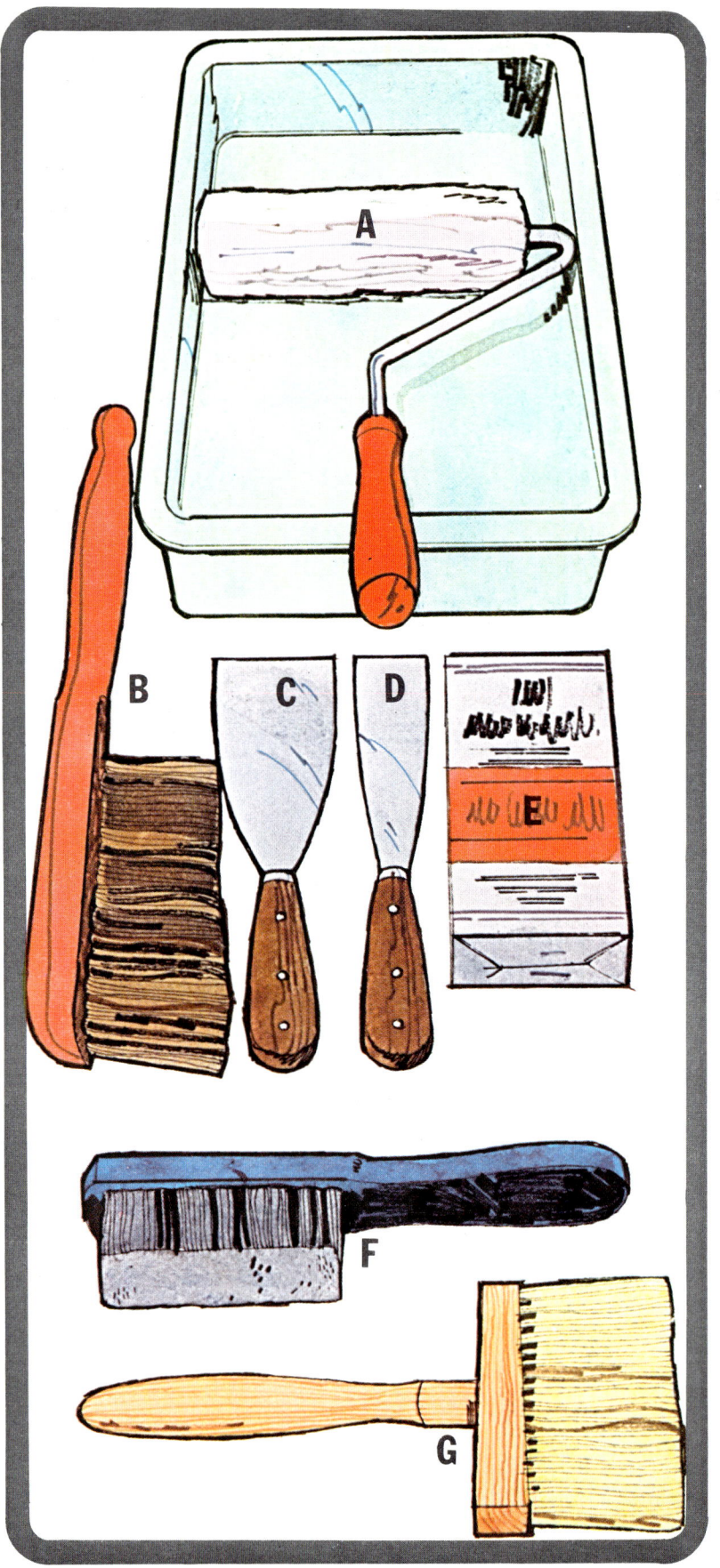

All old flaking and loose paint must be removed, *Fig. 1*, and the stiff bladed scraper **C** is used for this work. The whole area of wall, including scraped areas, is then firmly rubbed over with the stiff brush **F**, *Fig. 2*. Minor cracks and defects are then filled, using external plaster filler applied with the flexible bladed scraper **D**, *Fig. 3*.

Rubbing the hand brush **B** lightly over the repair will produce a smooth, blended finish. Where the surface of the wall is firm, the work described completes preparation except for a final rub over with a hand brush to remove dust.

Where initial repair reveals that the wall surface is in poor condition, then, after all surface material has been brushed away, a purpose made stabilising solution should be applied to prevent further flaking and powdering.

Fungicide

If, during the course of preparation, moss, lichen or other plant growth is found to be present on the walls, then this must be completely removed by scraping and brushing. It is also advisable to wash the walls down with a fungicide in order to kill any further growth which can quickly ruin an otherwise good finish.

Fungicide is available in liquid form and, as with paints and primers, must be used strictly in accordance with the manufacturers' instructions. Care must be taken during use to protect the eyes and skin.

Painting

For reasonably flat rendered areas a paint roller **A**, fitted with a mop type applicator, provides a quick and easy means of application for most types of paint. Where the wall surface is uneven, most types of brickwork for instance, then the long bristles of a wall type brush **G**, *Fig. 4*, will penetrate even quite deep undulations ensuring a good coverage of paint to the whole surface.

Dampness: Sources

With modern buildings, problems of dampness and rotting can generally be traced to a fairly simple defect, or lack of maintenance in waterproofing, of the water disposal system. Modern building regulation requirements ensure that a general high standard is maintained during initial building work, but even the best materials and systems require some maintenance if optimum performance is to be maintained.

A most important point with any outdoor defect is that it must be remedied at an early stage. Loose putty around a window, for instance, may appear quite trivial, but water will be constantly creeping in and soaking the unseen part of the frame. This type of constant dampness can quickly lead to rotting problems in timber and rusting with steel frames.

With older buildings, erected before stringent building controls were in force, walls were frequently built without a cavity or damp proof course or other moisture protection. With this type of building much can be done in the way of waterproofing the walls externally using purpose made protective paint, see page 86, and the lack of a horizontal damp proof course can be rectified by a specialised contractor 'injecting' a silicone damp course.

Flashings

Flashings around chimneys or roof windows can become displaced if the fixing mortar or nails deteriorate, or the flashing material perishes. A leakage at this point can go undetected for long periods, so a regular, say bi-annual, inspection should be made to check general condition.

Slates or Tiles

Cracked or broken roof tiles should be replaced without delay, see page 80, as, besides allowing water penetration, there is always the possibility of personal injury should a broken tile fall.

Window and Door Frames

The joint between frame and surrounding wall will often allow wind-blown rain penetration. A tubed type mastic compound, see page 76, can be used to seal this gap.

Loose or missing glazing putty around windows should be cut away and replaced, see page 76, but where the framework is damp this should be left to dry thoroughly before being re-prime painted and puttied.

Timber door and window ledges have a drip groove cut across the lower surface and this must be kept clear to prevent water running to adjacent walls.

Guttering and Downpipe

Leaks at guttering joints, see page 81, create a constant drip or stream of falling water which can soak into nearby walls or quickly break through protective paint coats. Overflowing guttering may be caused by a blocked downpipe preventing the escape of water build-up. A simple check can be made by examining the downpipe outlet when the gutter is overflowing. This problem is also sometimes caused by the gutter being incorrectly placed in relation to the roof tile edge, allowing water to 'jump' the gutter as it discharges from the roof.

Joints in gutter downpipes are not sealed and a blockage in the pipe will cause an overflow at the joint immediately above. This may be cleared using a wire hook or plunger, see page 80.

Damp Proof Course

A frequent problem here is where earth or other material is piled against the wall and over the damp course.

Dampness: Effects

Internal dampness problems with modern buildings are generally the result of faults in external weatherproofing or seals. With older buildings the fault may lie with poor construction. Some common sources of dampness are illustrated and described on page 88.

Another frequent internal dampness problem is that of condensation forming on walls and windows. Here modern buildings can be affected as well as old.

Ceilings

Damp patches on ceilings immediately under a roof can indicate a loose or broken roof tile or a damaged or misplaced flashing. Where water starts dripping through, possibly accompanied by a bulge in the ceiling plasterboard, then this could mean a leak in the roof space located water storage tanks or pipework. The first reaction here should be to turn on all taps in the house and flush lavatories in order to reduce the volume of stored water, then to turn off the water at the main stop cock, before calling assistance.

Walls

Damp patches on walls may be caused by a broken or loose roof tile near the edge of the building allowing water to soak down the wall. The problem may also be caused by an overflowing gutter or a leak in the rainwater down pipe. A damp patch low down could be the result of earth banked against a wall, bridging the damp proof course.

Doors and Windows

Damp areas around the sides and edges of doors and window frames may be caused by wind-driven rain penetrating between the frame and surrounding brickwork or around an ill-fitting door or window, or possibly running across the underside of a sill. Where water gathers in pools on the window ledge, the cause could be loose or broken glazing putty, but where water forms on the glass and runs down, the cause will be condensation.

Floors

Dampness on floors may be caused by leaks in the plumbing, possibly a waste trap under a sink or central heating pipework or valves. Where dampness forms on a solid floor, condensation could be the cause or, with an old building, a damp proof course may not have been fitted.

Condensation

When air comes into contact with a cold surface it gives up water in the form of condensation. The cause of the problem lies with inadequate heating, ventilation, thermal insulation or a combination or all three. Household condensation problems usually occur in kitchens and bathrooms, where additional moisture is produced through cooking and bathing. The fitting of an electric extractor fan to improve ventilation for the relatively short periods of use, often provides an answer.

Condensation dampness on cold walls in little used rooms can only be reduced through adequate heating and improved thermal insulation.

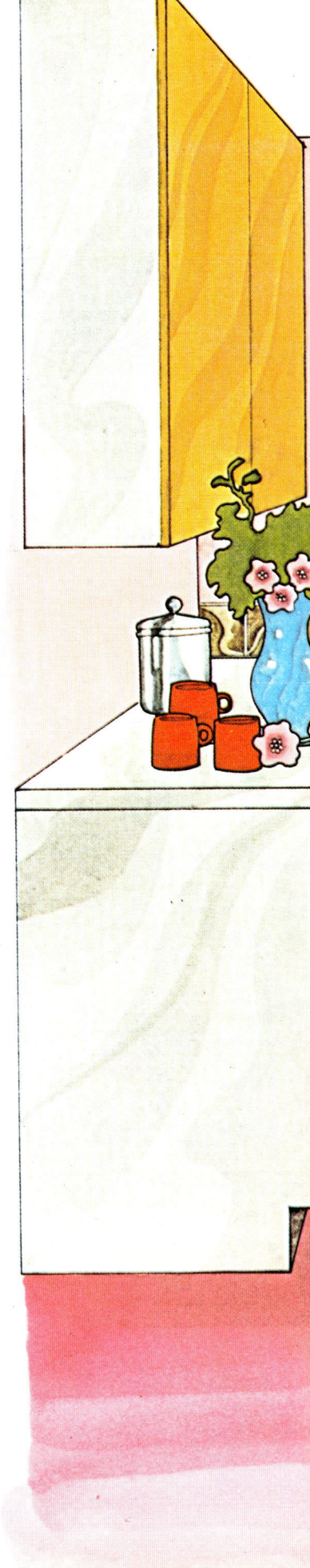

Concreting and Bricklaying: Paths and Drives

Concreting and bricklaying work falls well within the scope of home D.I.Y. provided the essential elementary skills are mastered and the correct tools are available. For the newcomer to this type of work, practice and familiarity of materials and tools can be achieved by tackling the work in stages. Laying a path or drive, for instance, involves all the important aspects of concreting work. Once a job of this type has been successfully carried out it is a simple step to the more complicated work of laying foundations for brickwork and buildings.

Building walls or buildings from bricks or building blocks is again work that can only be successful with practice. For the beginner, initial work here should be confined to non-structural garden walls and the like, where the necessary experience in handling both tools and materials can be gained, before structural work is tackled.

Concrete Mixes

Concrete consists of a mixture of cement, sand, stones and water mixed together in proportions according to the type of work involved. Sand and stones (aggregate) can generally be purchased conveniently as 'all-in' ballast, 20 mm ($\frac{3}{4}$ in) ballast being suitable for most paths and drives.

A strong mix suitable for paths and drives subject

heavy surface wear is: 1 part cement to 5 parts 'all-in' ballast, by volume.

A weaker mix suitable for paths, drives and floors subject to minimal wear is: 1 part cement to $6\frac{1}{2}$ parts 'all-in' ballast, by volume.

Mixing must always be carried out on a clean and flat surface. The dry ingredients should be thoroughly mixed, using a *clean* shovel **A**, clean water

being added to produce a stiff but workable mix.

Where large quantities of concrete are required, i.e. over about 2 cubic metres, then this is best purchased 'ready mixed', or a power concrete mixer may be hired for on-site mixing. A garden wheelbarrow is useful for site movement of mixed concrete.

Initial Preparation

Roughly mark out the area of the work and remove all surface vegetation. Approximate levels should next be checked using a timber straightedge **B**, together with a spirit level **C**. The area should be levelled and the top 50 mm (2 in) to 100 mm (4 in) of loose soil removed.

Shuttering

Lengths of timber, termed 'shuttering', are next laid to the edges of the work along lines set out by the timber pegs **D**, a club or lump hammer **E** being a suitable tool for driving these in. A bricklayer's line (strong twine) **F** is then stretched between the pegs at the intended finished concrete level, and the shuttering fixed, as *Fig. 1*, by nailing to the pegs.

Where the length of concrete is flat a slight sideways slope should be built in to prevent rainwater puddles forming. A small block of timber slipped under one end of the straightedge can be used to determine the necessary adjustment to the shuttering, *see Fig. 2*.

Pouring the Concrete

With all shuttering secure and level, the concrete should be mixed and poured. Compacting is then carried out by tamping the surface with the edge of a board, the top edge of the shuttering being used as a guide, see *Fig. 3*. Where a smooth surface finish is required, a float trowel **G** may be used as *Fig. 4*, about one hour after the initial laying.

Raft Type Foundations

Raft type foundations provide an easily constructed base on which to build a brick or timber workshop or garage.

Preparation

Mark out the area of the base, using the pegs **A** positioned so that the line **B**, stretched between them, marks the outline of the foundation. The base will be square when the diagonal measurements correspond, *Fig. 1*.

Clear away the top soil to a depth of about 150 mm (6 in), and dig the outer edge to a total depth of about 250 mm (10 in) × 150 mm (6 in) wide. Fix the shuttering **C** and **D** using a spirit level to transfer the corner locations from the lines to the shuttering timbers and to ensure a flat top surface. Use a broken brick infill to leave a concrete depth of approximately 75 mm (3 in) to 100 mm (4 in) over the central area, *see Fig. 2*.

A concrete mix of 1 part cement to 6 parts of 20 mm ($\frac{3}{4}$ in) all-in ballast is then poured, tamped and levelled, see page 92. A brick building may be built directly on top of the base, as illustrated, but rag bolt anchorages will be required for a timber building.

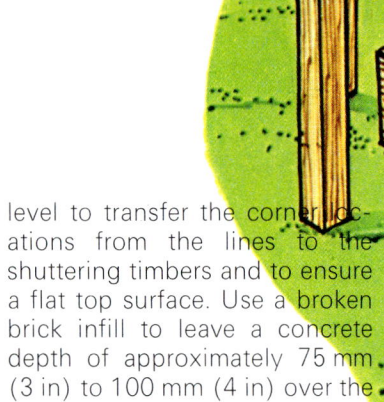

fig 2

Building

Concrete

Hardcore Infill

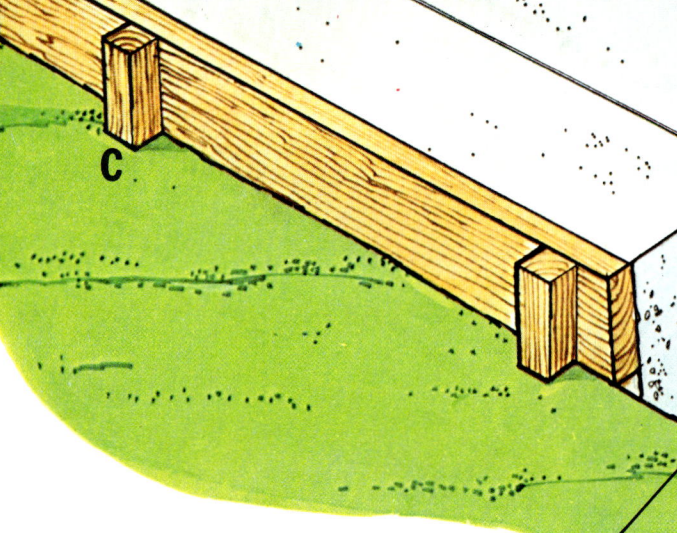

Hardcore Infill

Concrete

fig 1

Strip Type Foundations

The standard concrete foundation used for general house building work is the strip type illustrated. This consists of a concrete slab cast *in situ* in a trench dug along the main lines of the walls of the intended building.

The concrete slab presents a base on which the whole weight of the building will rest and, therefore, it must be adequate in width, generally about 600 mm (2 ft), and thickness, generally about 225 mm (9 in). Accuracy and depth of the foundation trench is also important and this will vary depending on site and ground conditions. Building work of this type generally requires local authority approval and inspection.

Setting Out

Profile boards, as *Fig. 1*, are set out to all corners of the intended building, as *Fig. 2*, with nails driven in to the horizontal member to represent the location of the walls of the building; twine, stretched between the nails, is then used to mark the complete wall layout. Diagonal measurements between opposing corners should correspond when the layout is exactly square.

Datum Peg

Before trench excavation is started a datum peg **A** must be driven into the ground to the damp proof course level of the intended building; this peg provides a base from which all depth measurements are subsequently taken.

The Trench

The foundation trench must be dug so that the walls will stand squarely in the centre, *see Fig. 2*, and a spirit level or plumb bob can be used to transfer the wall location from the twine marking lines to the ground. The excavation must be taken into firm subsoil, *see Fig. 1*, and the bottom and sides of the trench squarely and accurately dug. When firm sub-soil is reached, a spirit level **B** is used with a rule **C** to position the first foundation peg **D**. The top of **D** must represent the finished foundation concrete level and, in order to simplify subsequent bricklaying, must also accurately measure multiples of brickwork courses from the top of the datum peg **A**. Once **D** has been accurately set, a straight edge and spirit level is used to transfer the level to the next peg **E** — thence to **F** and so on, round the complete site. As a final check the last and first peg tops should correspond exactly.

Where the ground is sloping, steps may be included in the trench as *Fig. 1*. Again the difference in levels must be accurately represented in multiples of brickwork courses. The shutter board **G** is placed and secured by the pegs **H** to ensure a square and accurate step. The accuracy of peg **J** is established using the spirit level positioned on peg **D** and in conjunction with the rule measuring down to the top of **J** in a similar way to that shown between pegs **A** and **D**.

Pouring the Concrete

A mix of one part cement to $6\frac{1}{2}$ parts of 20 mm ($\frac{3}{4}$ in) 'all-in' ballast is generally suitable. This should be poured directly into the foundation trench and tamped level to the peg tops.

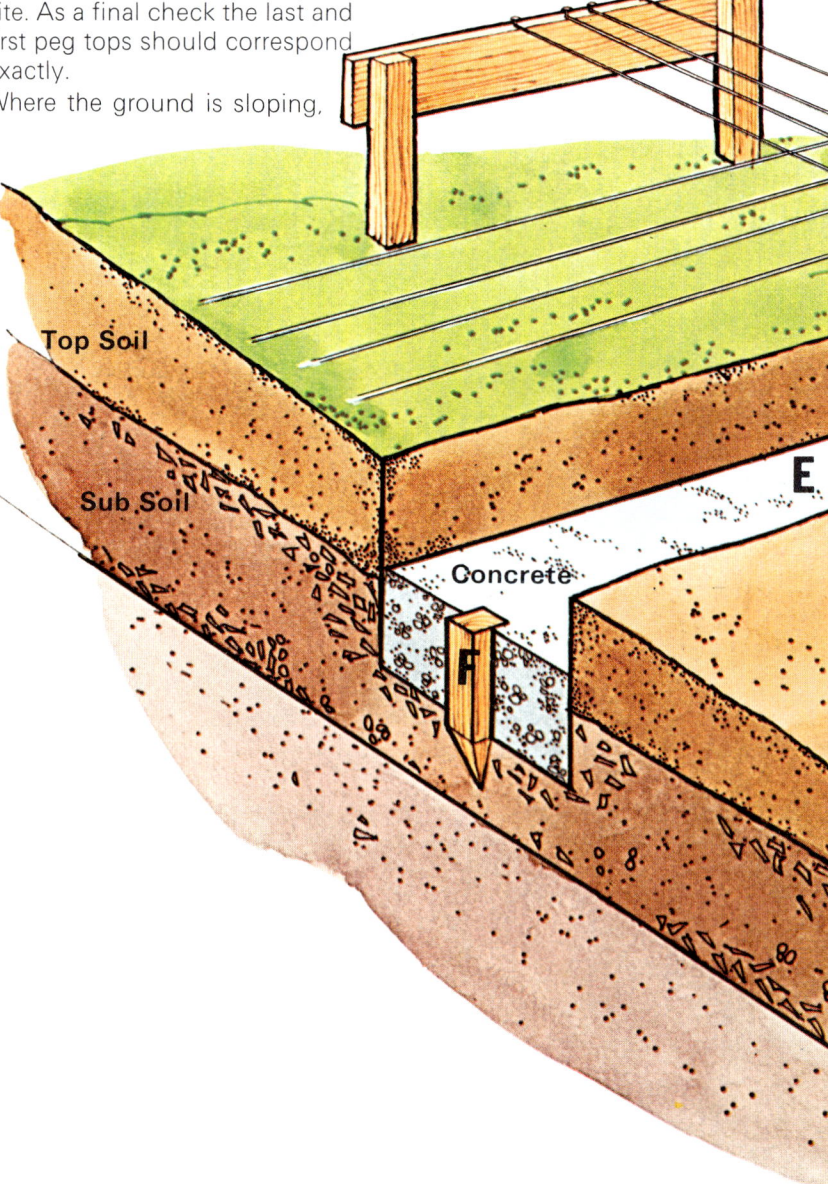

Top Soil

Sub Soil

Concrete

E

F

Concrete

Wall Location

fig 2

B

A

C

D

H

G

J

g1

Getting Started

Basic tools required for brick-laying are:

A *Clean* shovel with which to mix and transfer the mortar.

B Bricklayer's spirit level, at least one metre (3 ft) long, used constantly during the course of the work to ensure that the walls are perfectly vertical.

C Brick line (strong twine) to mark the wall locations between profile boards, *Fig. 1*, and also to use as a guide for the brickwork courses, *see Fig. 1*.

D. Bricklaying trowel with a 250 mm (10 in) blade. This type of trowel is often specially shaped with one straight and one slightly curved long edge. For a right-handed user the straight edge should be on the left of the blade. The edge of the blade can also be used in the form of a chopper for trimming corners and edges of bricks.

E Club or lump hammer, used

for general hammering work with timber pegs and also in conjunction with:

F a bolster, for cutting bricks.
G Line pins, used to secure line C to the brickwork.
H Joint rubbing tool consisting simply of a piece of 15 mm ($\frac{1}{2}$ in) diameter pipe bent as shown. The peak of the bend is used to 'iron' a smooth finish to the mortar.

In addition to the tools shown, a measuring tape and home-made timber set square, for setting and trying corners, will be required; also a 'gauge' rod. This consists simply of a length of timber batten marked with the brick courses and used to ensure accurate alignment of courses.

Mortar Mix
Four parts building sand to one part cement will produce a general purpose mortar mix, and ease of working can be improved by the addition of a liquid plasticiser. Only sufficient mortar for one hour of work should be mixed, as after this time it will start to set.

The First Brick
Figure 1 illustrates the method of locating the corner bricks of the walls on the foundation concrete. Locations may be 'transferred' from the lines, using either a plumb bob or level **B**.

fig 1

Building Up

For ease of working, the mortar mix must be kept free from contamination with stones and other debris. Here a 'spot board', consisting of a hardboard or plywood sheet approximately 600 mm (2 ft) square, should be placed near the work and the mortar transferred in small quantities from the main mix.

Types of Brickwork
Brickwork may be single skin, **Figs. 1 and 2** , suitable for a workshop, garage or low garden wall. For a high wall or a retaining wall a double thickness solid wall will probably be necessary. In deciding the type and thickness of a wall for specific application, many factors, such as site conditions, loadings, exposure to weather, and so on must be considered, and where doubts exist, professional assistance should always be sought.

Fig. 2 shows a single skin wall built up on a raft-type foundation as applied to a garage or workshop.

Fig. 3 shows a cavity wall construction, generally used in houses and other habitable buildings.

With the four corner bricks of the wall accurately located on the foundation concrete (see page 98), a complete line of bricks must next be laid around the perimeter. A second brick is laid at a distance measured to multiples of bricks and joints, allowing approximately 9 mm ($\frac{3}{8}$ in) for mortar joints, within the range of the spirit level. The level of the corner brick then can be transferred to the next brick by bridging the gap with the spirit level. After filling the gap, work can then proceed in leap-frog fashion until a complete line of bricks has been laid.

Figure1 illustrates the next step where the corners are built up to about six courses. Here the spirit level must be used frequently to ensure that the walls are truly vertical and flat; also the gauge, mentioned on page 98 should be used to ensure that the level of the courses proceeds accurately at all corners.

This method of building up the corners or ends applies to all types of work, e.g. buildings,

fig 1

garden walls, partition walls, in brick or blockwork, and represents the basis for an accurate and neat final job.

With the corners built up as *Fig. 1*, the brick line is next stretched taut to the top outer edge of the first infill course of brickwork. Flat bladed line pins (see page 98) being pressed into the mortar joint provide an anchorage point for the line, *see Fig. 1*. Where the distance between the corners is greater than about 4 metres (12 ft) then a centrally located brick should be laid as a line support and to prevent sagging.

Filling in is a matter of laying bricks to the line, which is then moved up as work proceeds, damp proof course and wall ties (with a cavity wall) being installed as necessary. After filling in is completed the corners are again built up as before and the work continued as described.

Pointing

A simple method of providing a neat and hard finish to the mortar joint is to use an 'ironing' tool, see page 98. In use the tool is used to rub a concave finish to the mortar joint. Pointing should be carried out as work proceeds and before the mortar sets too solidly.

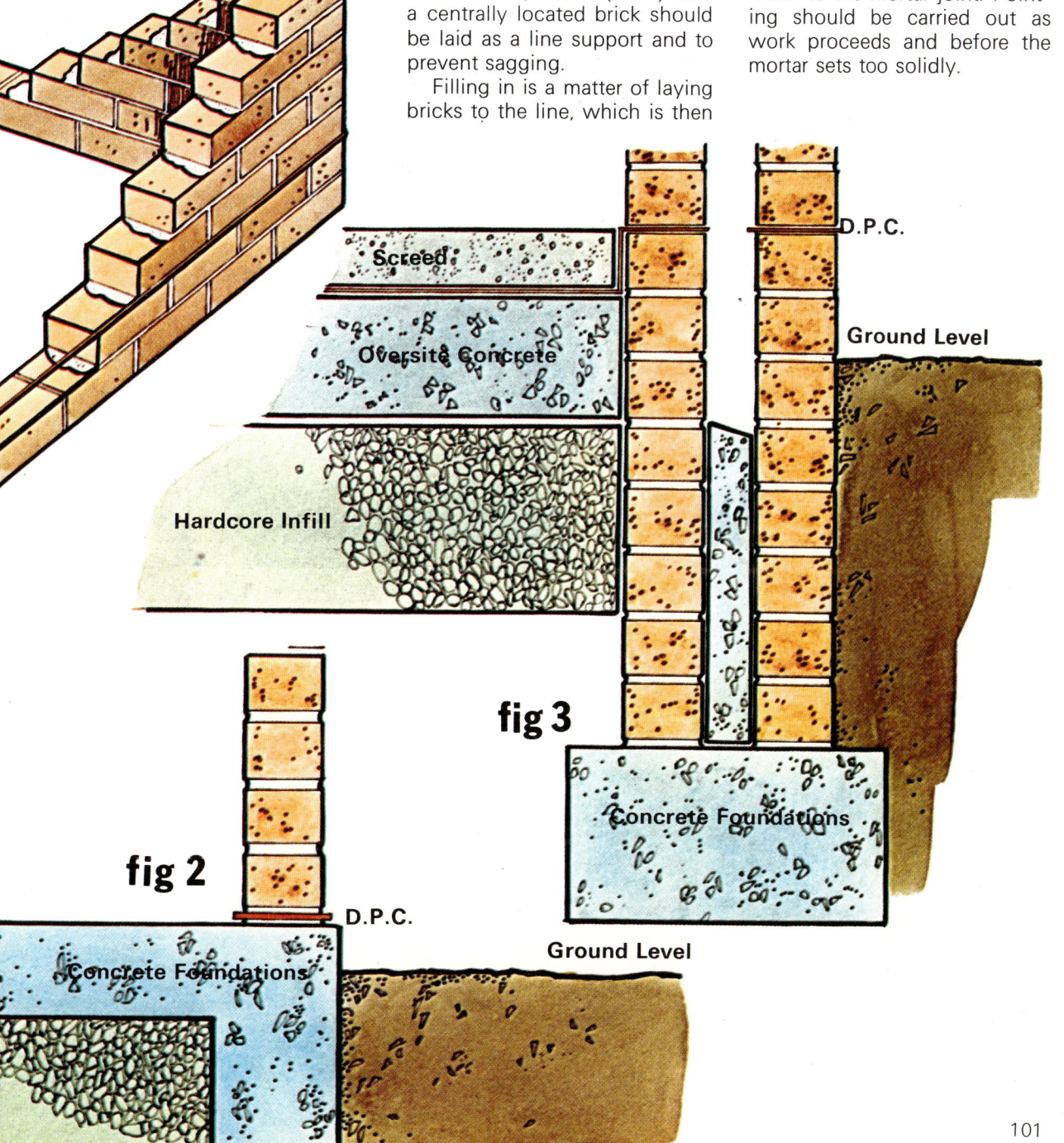

Screed

Oversite Concrete

Hardcore Infill

D.P.C.

Ground Level

fig 3

Concrete Foundations

Ground Level

fig 2

D.P.C.

Concrete Foundations

Fitting Doors and Window Frames

Window and door frames are available from specialist joinery manufacturers in a complete range of sizes, styles, shapes and types, but the method of fitting into the masonry shell of a building is generally similar for all.

As supplied, the frames will normally be painted with one coat of primer paint, and all concealed faces should be given a second coat before fixing. Frames are often supplied with *horns* left on the horizontal members to protect the corners in transit. These should be cut squarely away and the exposed wood thoroughly repainted. Frames are also sometimes supplied with a temporary timber stiffener fixed across the corners, again as protection during transit. These should be left in position until the frame has been fitted into the masonry. Before fitting any frame, carefully check to see that it is accurately square and true as a fault would be almost impossible to rectify once the masonry work is complete.

Subsequent door or window sash fitting would also be complicated with an out-of-true frame.

Door frames are normally fitted on a bed of mortar directly on top of the main damp proof course and when the brickwork is at this level. The frame is stood in position and temporarily but firmly supported by a stout length of timber nailed to the top, as **Fig. 1**. With the support in position a spirit level is used to set the frame truly vertical both from the front and side view. The brickwork is then continued up the sides of the frame with metal anchors being fitted to the sides at each third brickwork course, **Fig. 1**. The anchors are hammered into the woodwork of the frame and then flattened to the top of the brick

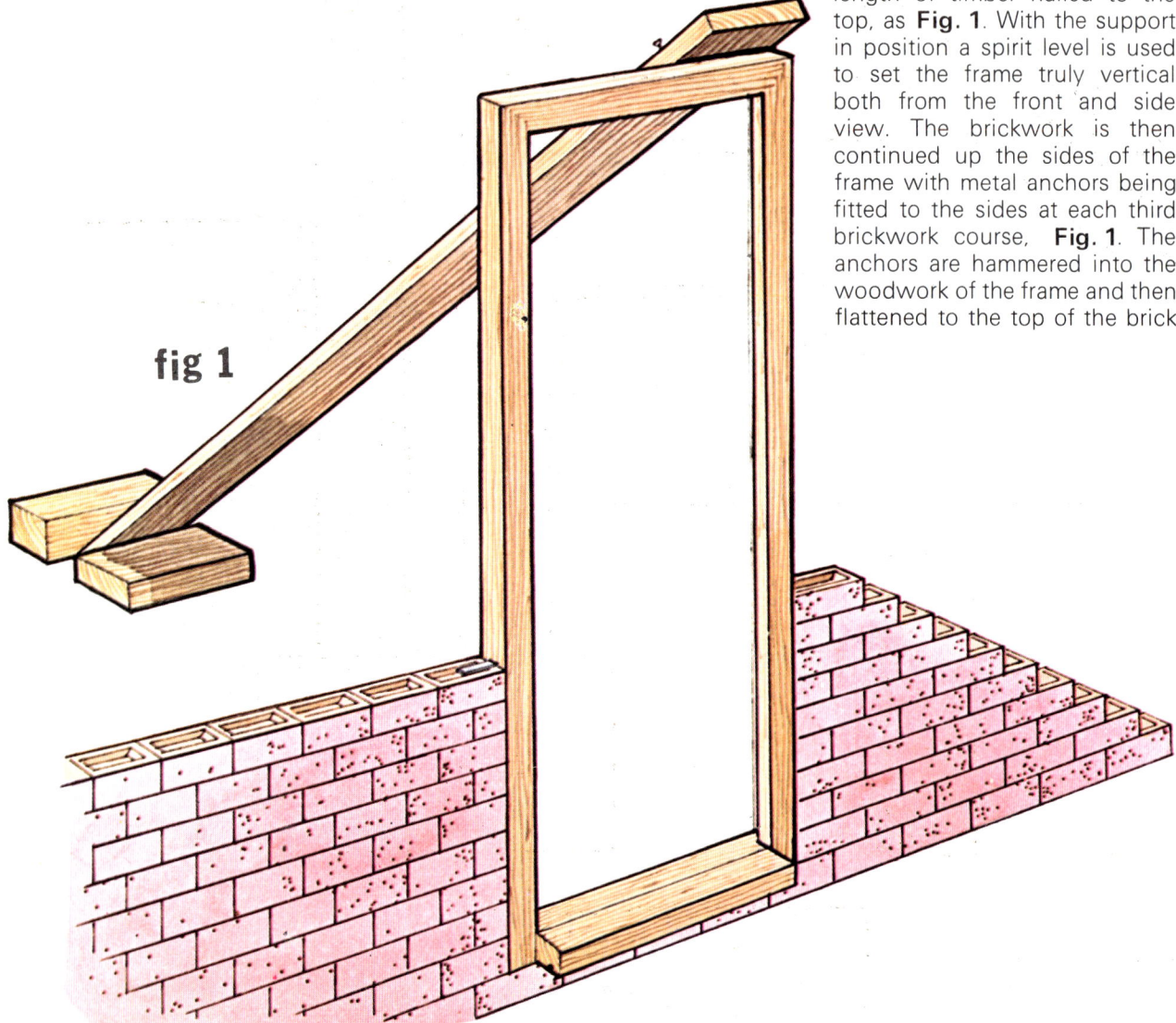

fig 1

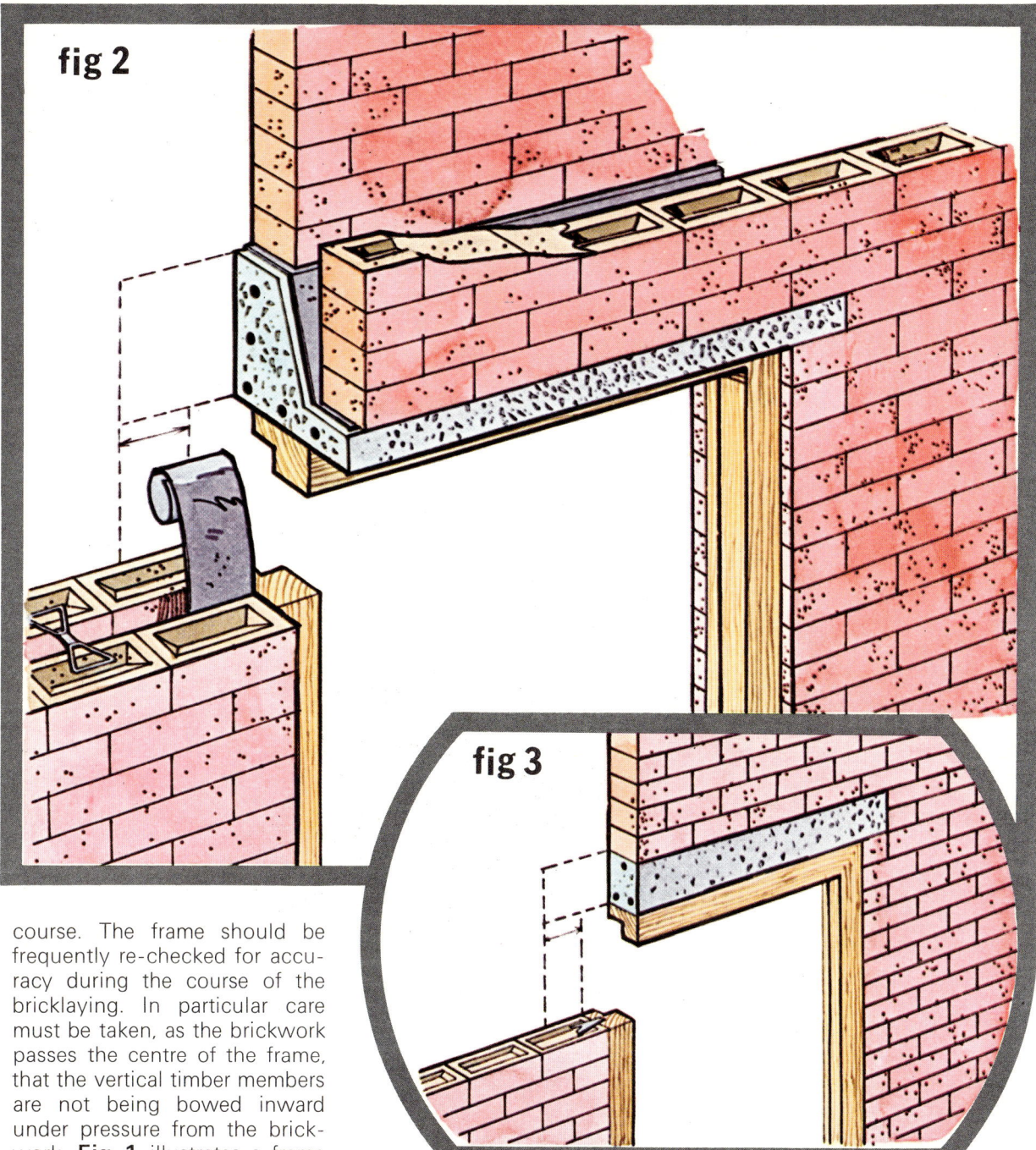

fig 2

fig 3

course. The frame should be frequently re-checked for accuracy during the course of the bricklaying. In particular care must be taken, as the brickwork passes the centre of the frame, that the vertical timber members are not being bowed inward under pressure from the brickwork. **Fig. 1** illustrates a frame in the course of fitting to single skin brickwork, and the method of fitting to a cavity wall is very similar except that the frame is generally recessed further into the opening, **Fig. 2**. Also with cavity brickwork a vertical damp proof course must be included as shown, where the inner wall returns to meet the outer.

Fig. 3 illustrates the method of bridging the brickwork over the door in a single skin building,

using a rectangular, steel-reinforced concrete lintel. The lintel must be at least 225 mm (9 in) oversize to the door opening to provide an adequate bearing on the brickwork to either side. Sectional dimensions will be governed by the width of the opening and the height and type of building.

Fig. 2 illustrates the method of using a 'boot' shaped, steel-

reinforced concrete lintel over an opening in a cavity wall. Again the lintel must be over-sized to the frame opening and of sufficient sectional size to cope with the loadings imposed. Here a flexible damp proof material is fitted over the lintel, and between the inner and outer walls, to ensure that any cavity moisture is channelled away from the inner wall.

Roofing

The layout of a gabled roof is considerably more complex than that of a flat roof and specialised skills in design and construction are necessary **Fig. 2** illustrates the basic parts of a pitched roof where the joists, **A**, run unbroken across the width of the building, resting on the inner skin of the cavity wall on a timber plate. The rafters, **B**, being securely nailed or bolted to the joist ends. Layout at this point varies with pitch and style of roof and a supplementary plate, **C**, is

Basically there are two main types of roof used in permanent buildings, the flat type, **Fig. 1**, and the gabled type, **Fig. 2**. Loadings imposed on a roof vary with the type of building, method of construction, exposure and many other factors. All must be taken into account at the design stage and in cases of doubt professional advice should be sought. This type of work will also generally be subject to local authority approval.

The Flat Roof: Fig. 1

Construction of the roof shown is by laying the rafters, **A**, in position, on top of the wall plate, **B**, which is set on top of the inner wall of the building and fixed with rag bolts. The rafters are skew nailed to the plate. The firring pieces, **C**, give the roof a weather slope and are nailed to the top of the rafters. The noggins, **D**, carry the roof neatly over the side walls. The fascia, **E**, is nailed in position to the noggins and then the main covering material, **F**, in the form of timber, chipboard or plywood fixed. Timber trim strips, **G**, are fitted to help to mould the felt covering for best weathering effect. The soffitt, **H**, is nailed to the underside of the rafter and noggin overhang.

The felt covering, **J**, is fitted direct to the main covering material.

fig 1

**Key to Flat Roof
(all parts timber except
where shown)**

FIGURE 1.

A	rafters
B	wall plate
C	firring pieces
D	noggins
E	fascia
F	main roof covering
G	timber trim strips
H	soffitt
J	felt covering (roofing felt)
K	plastic gutter
L	interior plasterboard
M	thermal insulation material

sometimes fitted to the top of the joists as shown. The rafters terminate at the ridge timber, **D**, which runs the complete length of the roof. Heavy timber purlins, **E**, also run the complete length of the roof to provide support to the centre of the rafter span. In addition most roofs also include vertical struts and horizontal ties to give further rigidity. The asbestos soffit, **F**, normally fits to a groove cut into the rear face of the fascia, **G**, and is held in position by the brackets, **H**. The fascia is nailed to the ends of the joists. Barge boards, **J**, are fixed to the ridge timber, fascia and stub noggins, **K**.

Weatherproofing consists of an underfelt, **N**, over which tile battens, **O**, are nailed. The tiles, **P**, are hooked and alternate course-nailed to the battens. The ridge tile, **Q**, set in mortar, neatly caps the peak.

Key to Gabled Roof
(all parts timber except where shown)

FIGURE 2.

A	joists
B	rafters
C	plate
D	ridge
E	purlin
F	soffitt (asbestos)
G	fascia
H	soffitt brackets
J	barge boards
K	noggins

L	ceiling plasterboard
M	thermal insulation
N	felt underlay
O	tile battens
P	concrete or clay roofing tiles
Q	Concrete or clay ridge tile
R	plastic gutter

fig 2

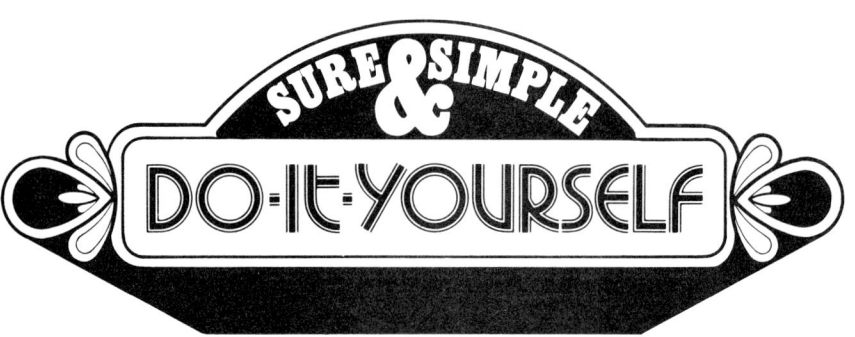

Plumbing: Domestic Hot Water System

Although household plumbing and drainage systems require little attention in the form of maintenance, the possibility of a breakdown caused by a leak, overflow or blockage is always possible. In particular every householder should be aware of the location and function of the main water supply and other shut down valves fitted to the water system. Also the location of inspection pits and rodding eyes in the drainage system.

A general working knowledge of the layout of the various systems can prove invaluable in diagnosing and tracing a fault. Trouble with plumbing can so often be traced to a sticking valve or other easily remedied problem, the repair of which may well be within the scope of the home handyman. In a case where a plumber must be called, an accurate description of the breakdown can often ensure that the necessary tools and parts are available, thus avoiding unnecessary delay.

Fig. 1 shows a standard modern indirect domestic water supply layout. Water is fed from the underground local water authority main, **A**, and is controlled externally by the authority's stop cock **B**. A householder's stop cock **C** provides internal control. The supply runs from this point direct to the drinking water tap **D** at the kitchen sink and also branches away to feed the main cold water reservoir tank, **E**. A further branch runs to the water heating system feed and expansion tank, **F**. The water level in both tanks is automatically governed by the floating ball valves, **G**. Cold water is supplied from tank **E** to the wash hand basin, bath and lavatory cistern. Cold water is also supplied from this tank to the hot water cylinder **L** where it enters at the bottom, is heated by the internal heat exchanger **M** and rises to the top by natural gravitation. Hot water is drawn off when basin, bath or sink taps are opened. A gate valve **N** is generally fitted to both cold feeds, allowing the supply to the taps to be turned off without draining the tank or cylinder.

Hot water is provided by the boiler **O** through a separate circuit. Hot water gravitates from the boiler, passes through the heat exchanger **M** where heat is passed to the tap supply, and then back to the boiler for re-cycling. Water in the tank **F** keeps the system topped up and caters for expansion and contraction as the water is heated and cooled. The vent pipes **P** prevent pressure build-up within the system and allow air to escape.

The domestic hot water and boiler circuits are separated as shown to minimise scaling which occurs with older type 'direct' water heating systems. Alternatively a 'self priming' type, employing an internal air lock water separation system, may be installed. With these types the tank **F** is not used.

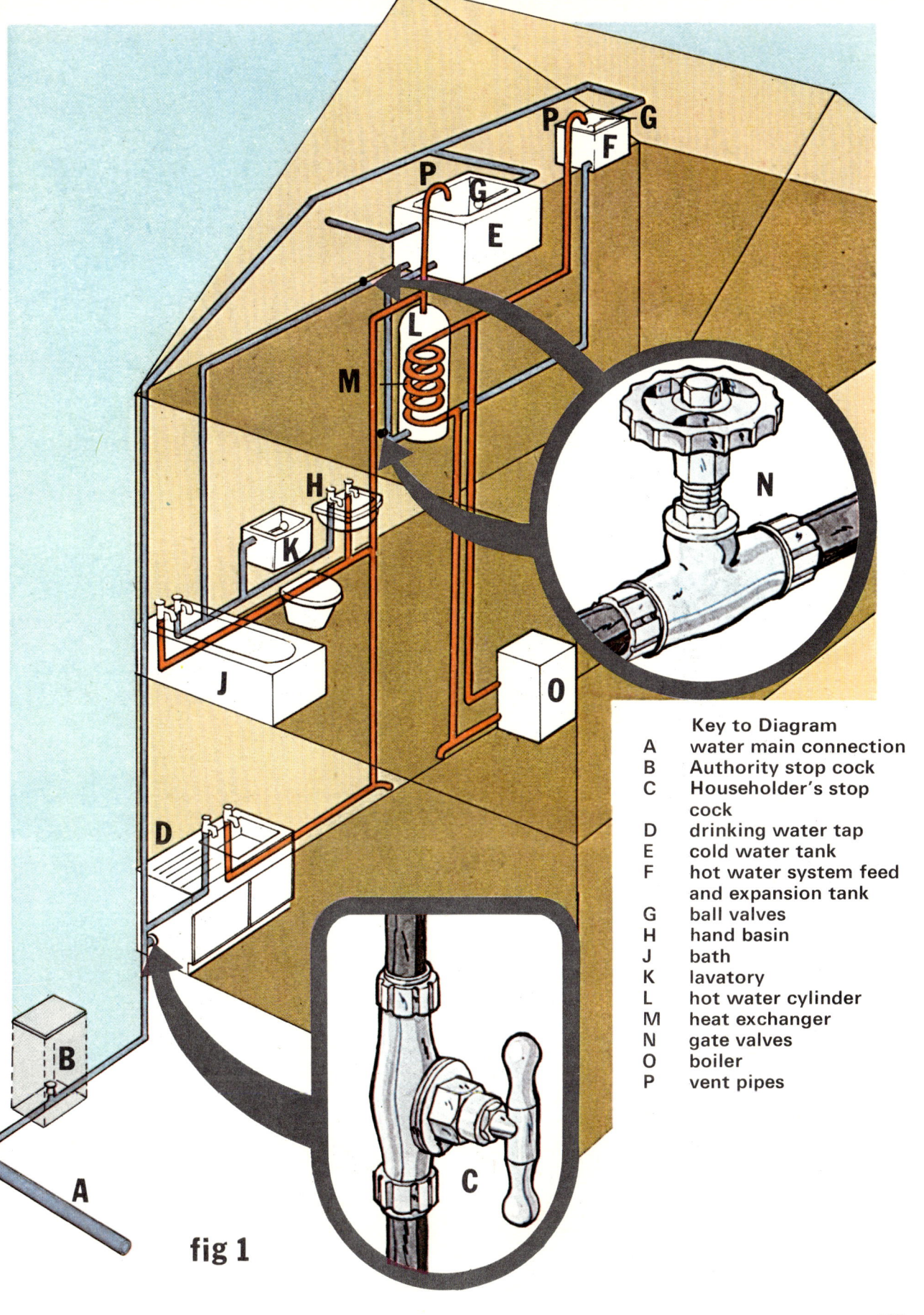

Key to Diagram

A water main connection
B Authority stop cock
C Householder's stop cock
D drinking water tap
E cold water tank
F hot water system feed and expansion tank
G ball valves
H hand basin
J bath
K lavatory
L hot water cylinder
M heat exchanger
N gate valves
O boiler
P vent pipes

fig 1

Central Heating System

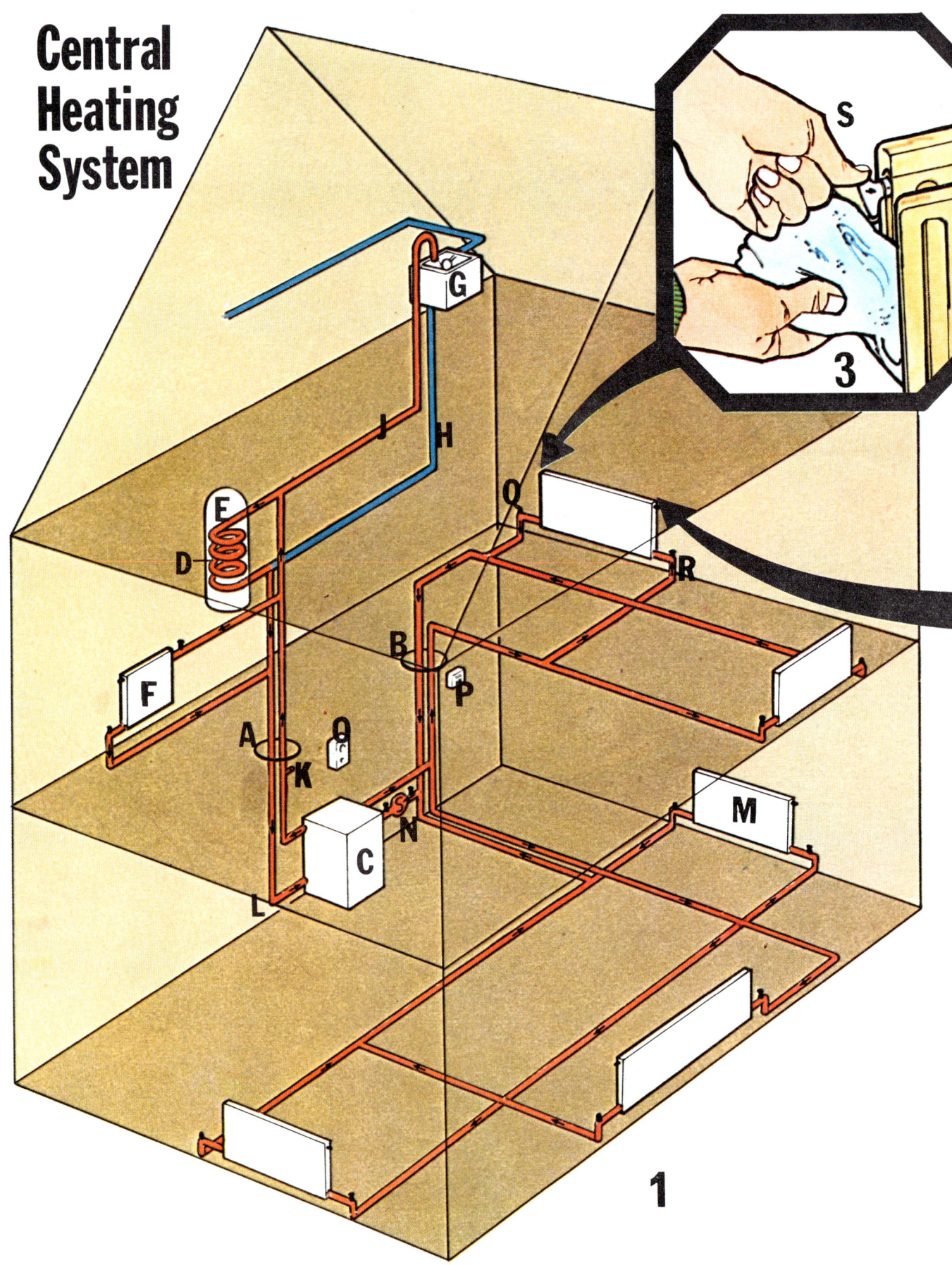

Fig. 1 illustrates the layout of a standard hot water/radiator central heating system as installed in many homes. The system consists of two main water circuits: the primary circuit **A** and the central heating circuit, **B**.

Key to Diagram

A primary circuit
B heating circuit
C boiler
D heat exchanger
E hot water cylinder

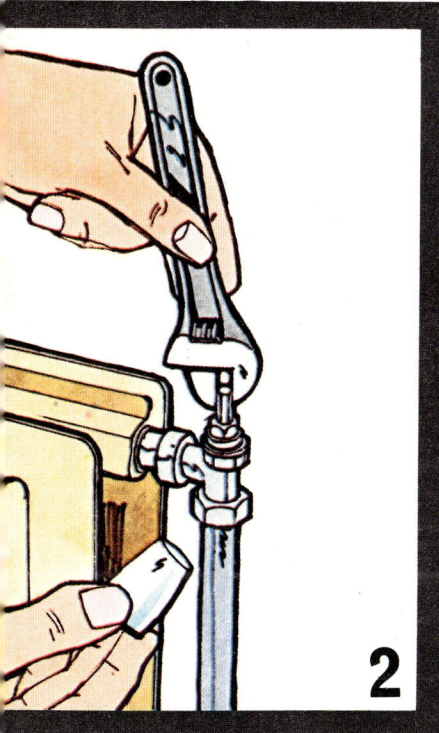

F bathroom radiator
G feed and expansion tank
H feed and expansion pipe
J vent pipe
K safety valve
L drain valve
M radiators
N pump
O programmer
P thermostat (air)
Q radiator hand valve
R lockshield valve
S air bleed valve

Primary Circuit

Water is heated in the boiler **C** from where it circulates by natural gravitation through the heat exchanger, **D**. Here heat is transferred from the primary water to the domestic hot water contained within the cylinder, **E**. Workings of the domestic hot water system are shown on page 106. The cooled primary water then returns to the boiler for re-heating. With most domestic systems this circuit includes a bathroom-located radiator or towel rail **F** through which hot water circulates, independently of the main central heating system, and whenever the boiler is running.

The feed and expansion tank **G** acts as a reservoir for automatic topping up of the heating system and also caters, through the feed pipe **H**, for expansion and contraction of water through temperature changes. The vent pipe **J** prevents pressure build-up in the system and also acts as a ventilation point for any air in the system. A spring loaded pressure valve **K** is generally fitted to the primary flow pipe as a safety precaution in the event of a blockage or overheating.

A system drainage valve, with hose pipe connection adaptor, is generally fitted at point **L** or within the boiler casing.

Radiator Circuit

The central heating circuit works by water passing through the pipework **B** to the radiators **M** where heat is given off into the rooms. The cooled water then returns to the boiler for re-heating. Because of the complexity of the pipe runs, the water will not circulate by natural gravitation alone and an electrically driven accelerator (or pump) **N** is therefore included in the return circuit to ensure effective water movement. Gate valves are fitted to the pipework either side of the pump to facilitate replacement or maintenance, without the need to drain the pipework. The output or 'head' of the pump is adjustable to suit the requirement of the system.

Control

Most completely automatic heating systems are either gas or oil fired and main control is achieved through a time switch/programmer **O** wired into the electricity supply to the boiler. The function of the programmer is to switch the boiler and central heating on and off at pre-set times, and control over the domestic hot water is effected simply by switching the boiler on and off.

Control over the central heating is effected primarily by the programmer being wired into the electricity supply to the circulating pump **N** but also through an air temperature operated switch (thermostat) **P** which is also wired into the circuit after the programmer. The thermostat switches the pump on and off, independently of the programmer, when room temperature fluctuates above or below the setting.

In addition to the external controls described, the boiler is equipped with a built-in manual thermostat control which also acts as a safety switch to prevent overheating.

Radiators

On/off control on individual radiators is by a hand-operated valve **Q** which governs the flow of water into the radiator. A second 'lockshield type' valve **R** is fitted to the opposite end of the radiator. This valve is used as Fig. 2 to make semi-permanent 'balancing' adjustments to the system to ensure an even flow of water through the radiators. These valves may be situated at the top or bottom of the radiator depending upon the pipe work layout used. All radiators are also fitted with a key-operated air bleed valve, **S, Fig. 3**. from which air may be required to be released from time to time.

Drainage

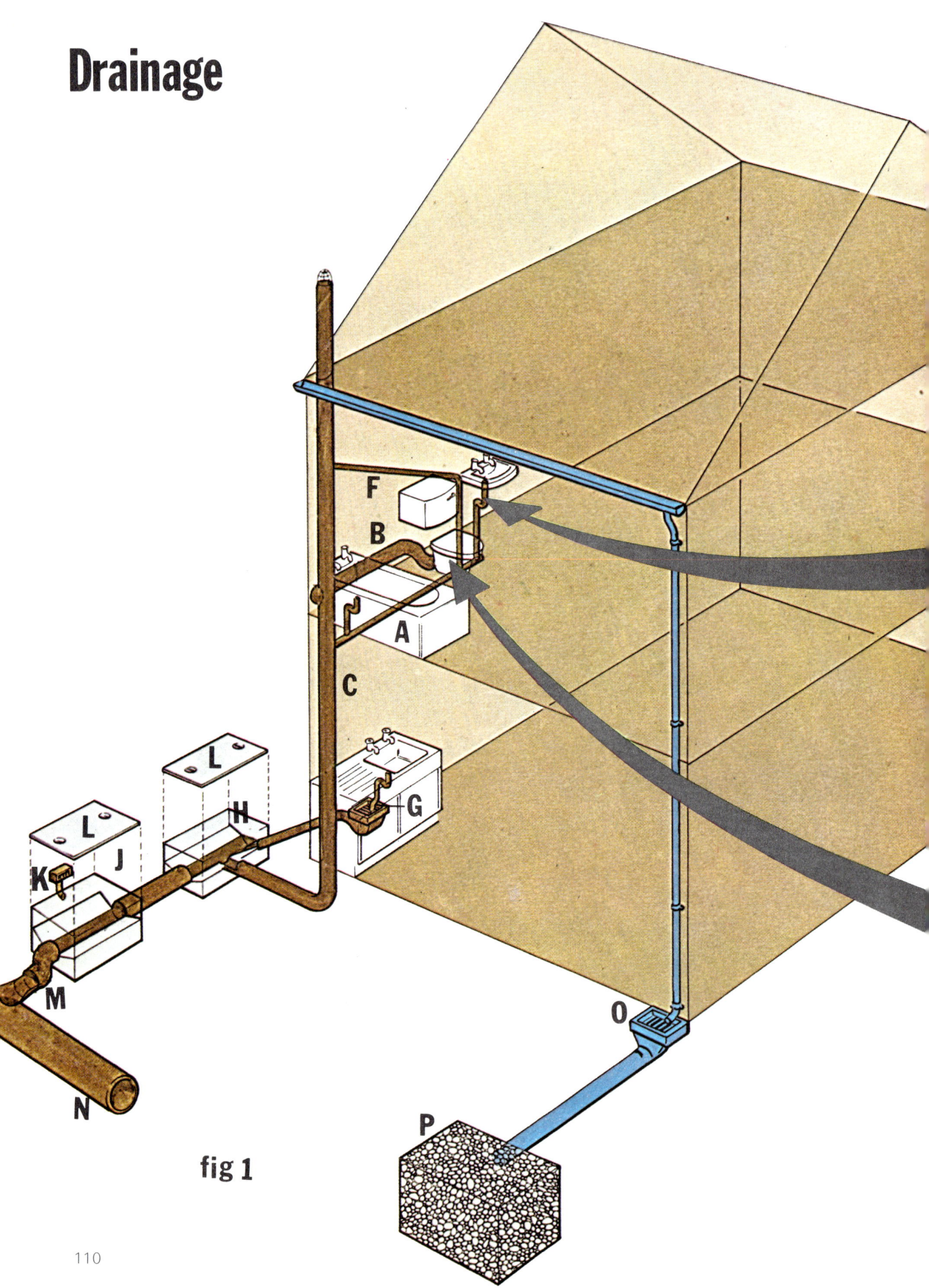

fig 1

Waste water from a house is usually disposed of through two completely separate drainage methods. The main system caters for what is known as 'foul' water drainage, and this consists of waste from sinks, basins and lavatories. The secondary system caters for surface or rainwater from roofs and driveways.

House drainage systems have changed considerably over recent years, with the old, open type of two pipe system being superseded by the modern single stack system, illustrated in **Fig. 1** Materials have also changed with the older cast iron, lead and stoneware, being replaced, almost exclusively, with plastic and pitchfibre pipework and fittings. With the modern system foul water from sinks, baths and lavatories is drained through plastic pipework **A** and **B**, to a single main stack, **C**. This stack terminates well above the roof of the house and is left open to the air as a ventilation point for the system. Smells are prevented from entering the house by water traps in the drainage pipes **D**, **Fig. 2**, and in the lavatory pan **E** **Fig. 3** Further protection is built in to many systems by an anti-syphon pipe **F** which prevents suction building up and possibly unsealing the water traps. Drainage from the kitchen sink is often through a gulley as shown, **G**.

The foul water runs from the house to an inspection chamber junction **H** and then on to a second inspection chamber **J** immediately prior to the main drainage connection point. An intercepting trap with rodding eye **M** is normally installed at the outlet point of this chamber. The main drainage pipe **N** is connected to the local authority sewage works, where the foul water is treated and disposed of.

Rainwater from roofs is normally disposed of via a gulley **O** leading to a simple underground soakaway pit, **P**.

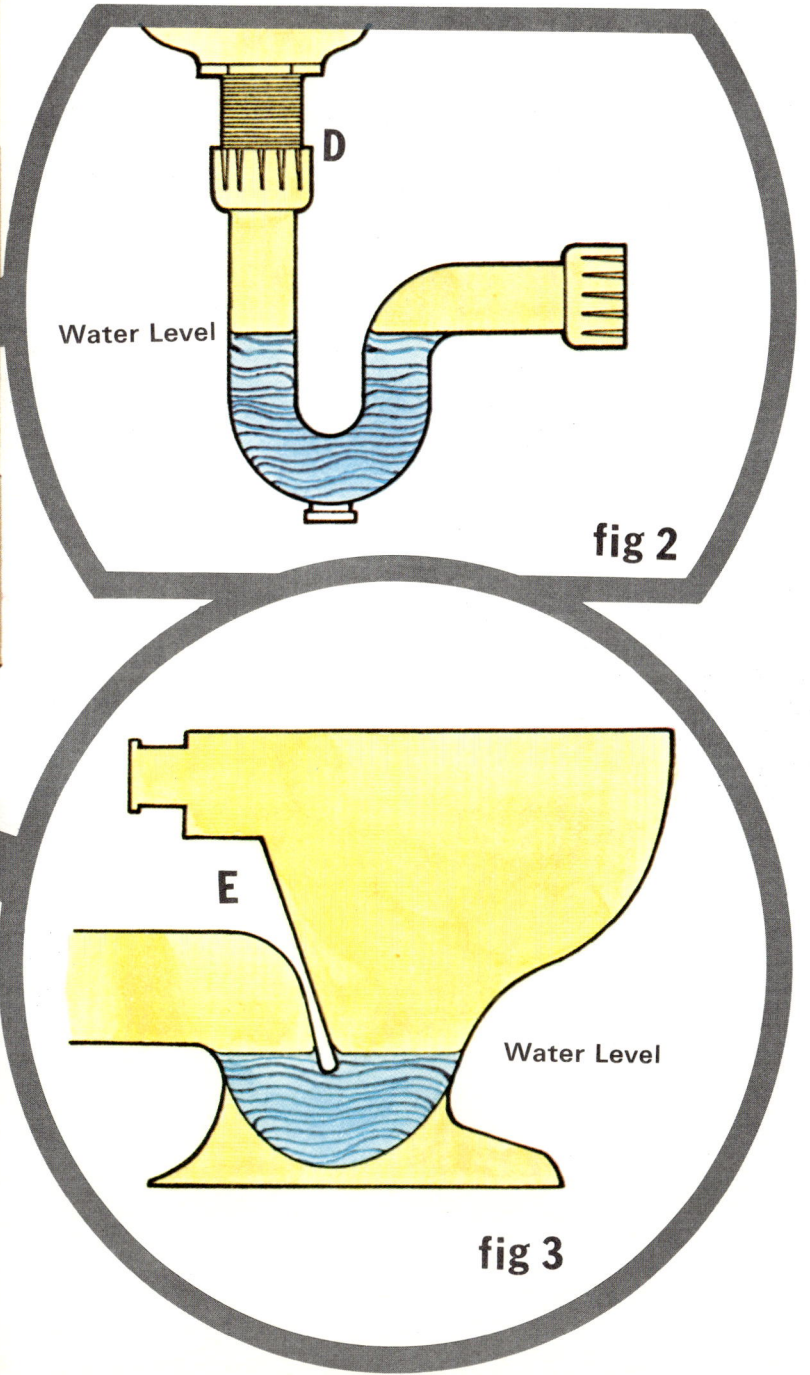

Water Level

fig 2

E

Water Level

fig 3

Key to Diagram

A	sink and bath drain pipe
B	lavatory drain pipe
C	main stack
D	water trap
E	toilet water trap
F	anti syphon pipe
G	gulley
H	inspection chamber
J	inspection chamber
K	air vent
L	airtight covers
M	intercepting trap
N	main drain
O	gulley
P	soakaway pit

111

Tools and Materials

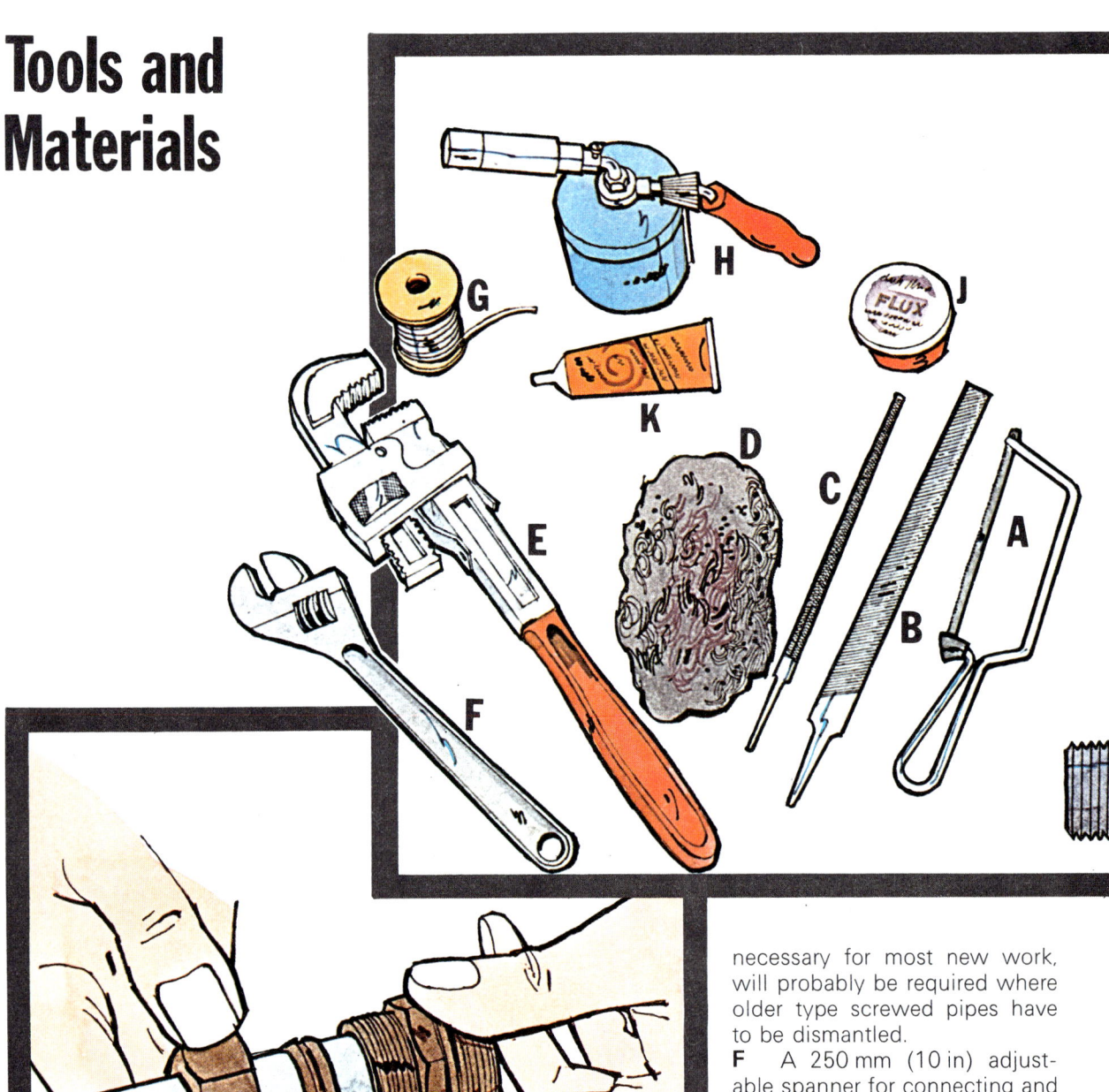

necessary for most new work, will probably be required where older type screwed pipes have to be dismantled.

F A 250 mm (10 in) adjustable spanner for connecting and disconnecting nut type parts and fittings, *Fig. 1*.

G, **H** and **J** Solder, gas blow lamp and flux for use with capillary type fittings, *Fig. 2*.

K Cement solvent for use with some types of plastic pipe.

Materials and Techniques

Modern pipe and plumbing fittings are available in either metal or plastic. Metal fittings are generally made from copper, stainless steel, brass or gunmetal and are used for high pressure and hot water services. Plastic pipe and fittings are used mainly for cold services and waste pipe. Special grades of

Most home plumbing maintenance and project work can be carried out with quite a modest tool kit. Main tools required are for cutting, cleaning up, and connecting.

A Junior hack saw consisting of a simple frame into which replaceable blades can be quickly fitted.

B Medium sized general purpose file for cleaning up the external ends of cut material.

C Circular or 'rat-tail' file for cleaning up internal ends of cut pipe.

D Medium coarse steel wire wool for polishing the mating surfaces of pipe and fittings immediately prior to assembly.

E An adjustable stilson wrench which, although not

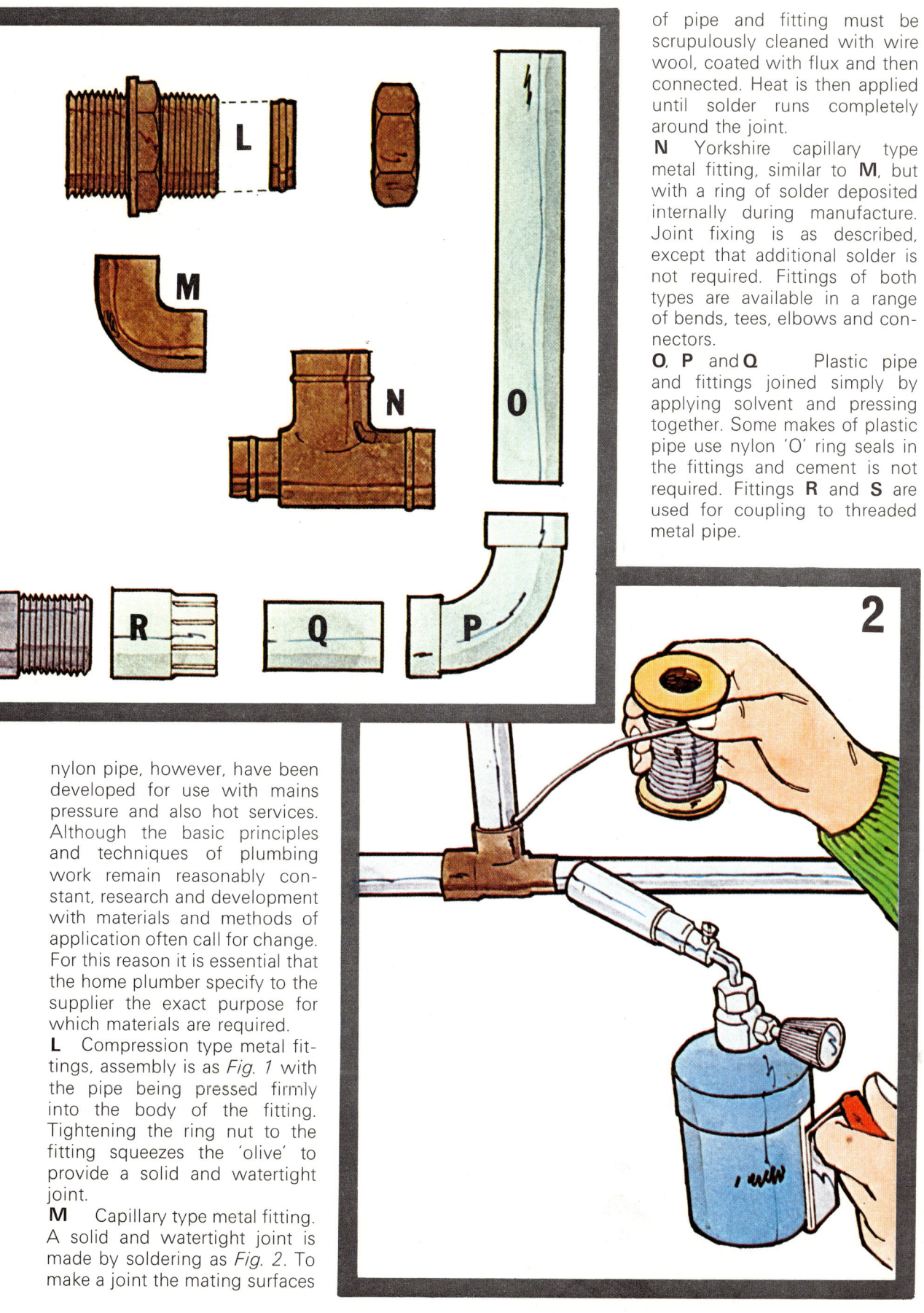

of pipe and fitting must be scrupulously cleaned with wire wool, coated with flux and then connected. Heat is then applied until solder runs completely around the joint.

N Yorkshire capillary type metal fitting, similar to **M**, but with a ring of solder deposited internally during manufacture. Joint fixing is as described, except that additional solder is not required. Fittings of both types are available in a range of bends, tees, elbows and connectors.

O, **P** and **Q** Plastic pipe and fittings joined simply by applying solvent and pressing together. Some makes of plastic pipe use nylon 'O' ring seals in the fittings and cement is not required. Fittings **R** and **S** are used for coupling to threaded metal pipe.

nylon pipe, however, have been developed for use with mains pressure and also hot services. Although the basic principles and techniques of plumbing work remain reasonably constant, research and development with materials and methods of application often call for change. For this reason it is essential that the home plumber specify to the supplier the exact purpose for which materials are required.

L Compression type metal fittings, assembly is as *Fig. 1* with the pipe being pressed firmly into the body of the fitting. Tightening the ring nut to the fitting squeezes the 'olive' to provide a solid and watertight joint.

M Capillary type metal fitting. A solid and watertight joint is made by soldering as *Fig. 2*. To make a joint the mating surfaces

Maintenance and Repairs

Most plumbing problems consist of minor faults, such as a sticking valve, leaky washer or blocked waste trap, all comparatively simple jobs that can be repaired with a minimum of tools.

Fig. 1 illustrates a cold water storage tank, normally situated in the roof space of a house. Most plumbing systems will be equipped with two such tanks. The functions of both are described on pages 106. Connec-

time to time to keep them free and in good working order.

Taps

The main drinking water tap at the kitchen sink generally gets heavy use and consequently the washer requires frequent renewal. After the mains supply has been turned off at the internal stop cock, see page 106, the standard pillar tap can be stripped as **Fig. 2** and the washer, fitted to the jumper,

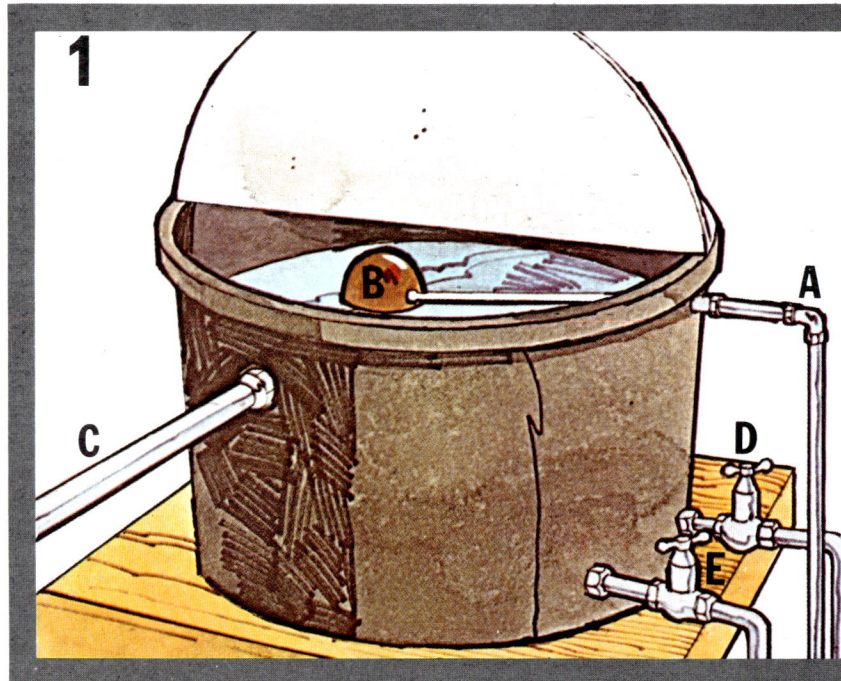

tions to the tank are **A**, the main cold water feed, controlled by the floating ball valve, **B**. The connection **C** is a safety overflow pipe channelling water outdoors in the event of ball valve failure, a problem which normally occurs if the system has not been used for some time. Here corrosion from minerals in the water can build up, causing the valve to lock either in the closed or open position. Normally cleaning away the corrosion will restore the valve to full operating condition.

The cocks or valves, **D** and **E**, control cold water supplies to the domestic cold water and domestic hot water systems. The heads should be turned from

renewed. Unscrew the domed cover by hand and lift up to expose the main head gear which is removed using a spanner.

Where a Supa-tap is fitted this can be stripped as **Fig. 3**. Unscrew the nut above the nozzle with a spanner and then unscrew the nozzle assembly by hand. The jumper, with the washer, can be pressed out from the spout of the nozzle. With this type of tap it is not necessary to turn off the main supply.

Water Traps

A blocked or slow draining basin or bath is normally caused by debris wedged in the water trap.

With plastic bottle type traps, **Fig. 4**, the lower part of the trap can be unscrewed, with a bucket underneath to catch the inevitable water spillage, and the obstruction cleared; re-tightening must be by hand pressure only. Metal '**S**' or '**P**' traps usually include a screwed cap which can be removed to clear a blockage.

Radiator Removal

Redecoration can be simplified if radiators are first removed from the wall. Start by turning off both the hand and lockshield valves fitted to the radiator. Next place a bowl under one of the end unions, and loosen slowly, as **Fig. 5**, allowing the water to drain steadily into the bowl. After all water has drained, unscrew both unions and lift the radiator free. After reconnection, turn on the valves and open the air bleed valve to refill.

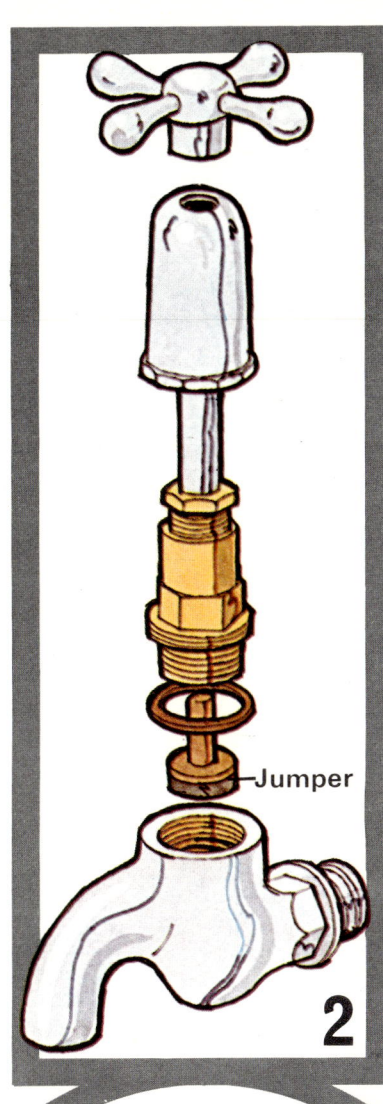

Jumper

2

4

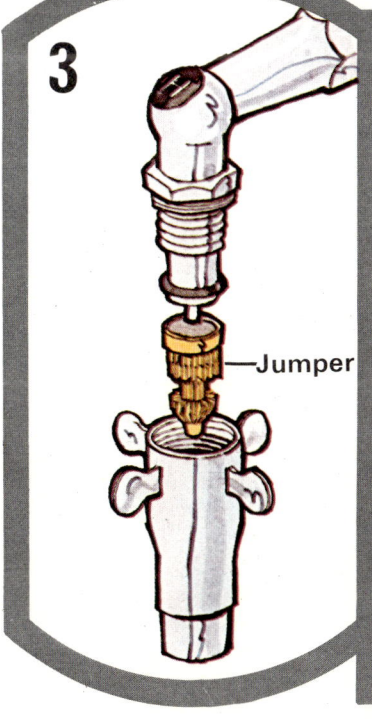

3

Jumper

5

Home Insulating

When the air temperature inside a house is raised above that of the outside air, heat starts to leak away through the various parts that make up the structure. Basically the rate at which the heat escapes is governed by the internal and external temperature differential, the greater this is the faster heat will be lost. In order to maintain a comfortable temperature in the house, heat must be produced continuously in order to replace heat escaping. In this way the cost of fuel consumed in heating is directly related to the rate at which heat is lost. The drawing opposite illustrates losses from a typical house.

Whilst it is not economically feasible to completely prevent this loss it is, nevertheless, possible to improve the position by reducing the loss rate. With most areas of heat loss an improvement can be made by adding a layer of insulating material to the existing structure. For this purpose various methods and materials are employed, depending on the structural material involved. In most cases the insulating method or material creates an area of relatively still air between the warmth of the house and the chill of outdoors. The blanket, **Fig. 1**, or granulated material, **Fig. 2**, for instance, used extensively to reduce heat loss through the roof of a house, contain large volumes of trapped air.

Savings

The economics of insulating are directly related to fuel costs; as these rise so the economical insulation investment also rises. Generally, initial outlay can be recovered through fuel savings within a reasonable period, after which the return represents a permanent saving.

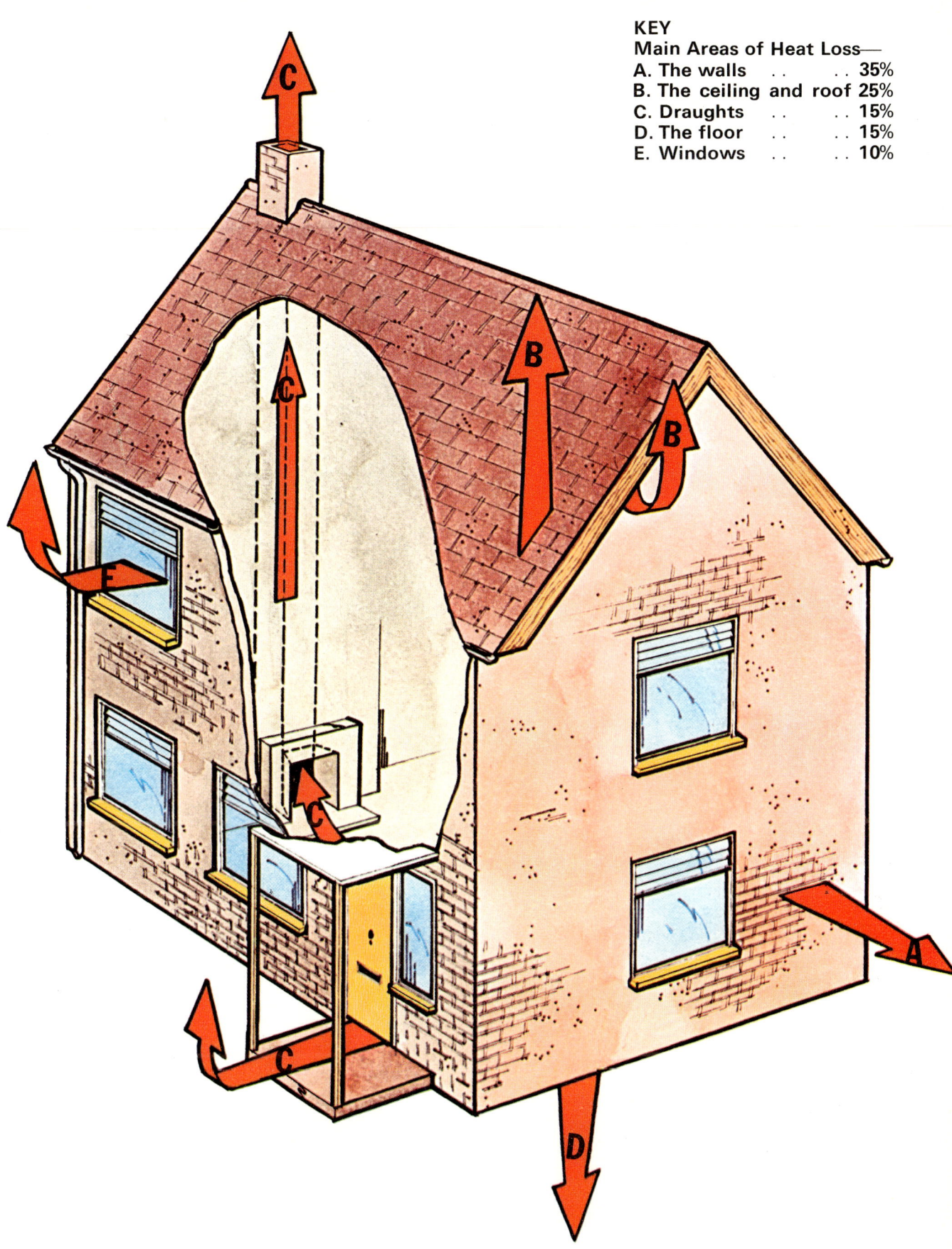

KEY
Main Areas of Heat Loss—
A. The walls 35%
B. The ceiling and roof 25%
C. Draughts 15%
D. The floor 15%
E. Windows 10%

Home Insulating Techniques

1

2

3

Few windows and doors are completely draught proof, and many, especially much used front and back doors, allow large volumes of expensively heated air to be lost in the form of draughts. Infrequently used hinged doors and windows can be quickly draughtproofed using a self adhesive foam plastic strip. **Fig. 1**. The strip is stuck in position so that the hinged part of the window or door closes squarely against it.

With doors and windows subject to heavy use, a metal or plastic clad excluder, **Fig. 2**, screwed or nailed to the reveal of the frame, provides an effective and durable seal. Other sources of draught losses are fixed ventilators. These can be replaced with an adjustable air register as a means of controlling ventilation. Open throated chimneys present a major heat loss and, where the chimney is not used, the throat should be restricted. Where the chimney is used, draught losses can be drastically reduced by fitting a room-sealed fire, **Fig. 3**.

Walls

With most buildings, the standard solid or cavity brick external walls make up a major area of heat loss. Insulating a cavity wall involves pumping either foam or wool material into the cavity, an operation in which the skill and equipment of a specialised contractor are necessary.

Fig. 4 illustrates the normal foam injection process. The insulation of solid walls can be improved by the fitting of an internal false wall. Here timber battens are fixed to the existing wall, **Fig. 5**, the cavity filled with insulating material and then a sheet cladding fitted to the battens. With this method, reflective aluminium foil can be fitted under the battens as an alternative to insulation blanket or sheet material.

Double Glazing

Heat loss through glass can be reduced by a secondary window fitted to trap an air 'buffer' between the warm inside air and cold outdoor air. Various methods can be used.

Sealed Units

These consist of two sheets of glass, edge-sealed with an air

trap cavity between, and designed to be fitted in the same way as traditional single glazed windows.

Dual Glazing

With this system a plastic or metal frame is fitted to a second pane of glass fixed by clips to the existing window frame, **Fig. 6**. **Fig. 7** illustrates a similar system where hinges are used in place of clips.

Double Windows

With this type, either hinged, **Fig. 7**, or sliding, **Fig. 8**, secondary windows are fitted to a complete frame fixed in the window reveal.

Floors

A good quality underlay under all ground floor carpets will considerably reduce heat loss through the floor.

Electricity

The colour code for the electrical wiring described in the book is that used in the U.K. Readers in Australia and New Zealand should note that their code is as follows:—

RED–LIVE, BLACK–NEUTRAL, GREEN—EARTH

It is a requirement in Australia and New Zealand that all electrical fittings must be installed by a competent and qualified person.

SURE & SIMPLE DO·IT·YOURSELF

For the untrained householder, home electrical work should be confined to simple jobs such as changing a fuse or fitting a plug. Alterations, repairs and extensions to the main wiring system call for special skills and this work is best entrusted to a qualified electrician. In any event this type of work should be inspected and approved by the local Electricity Authority before final connections to the main supply are made.

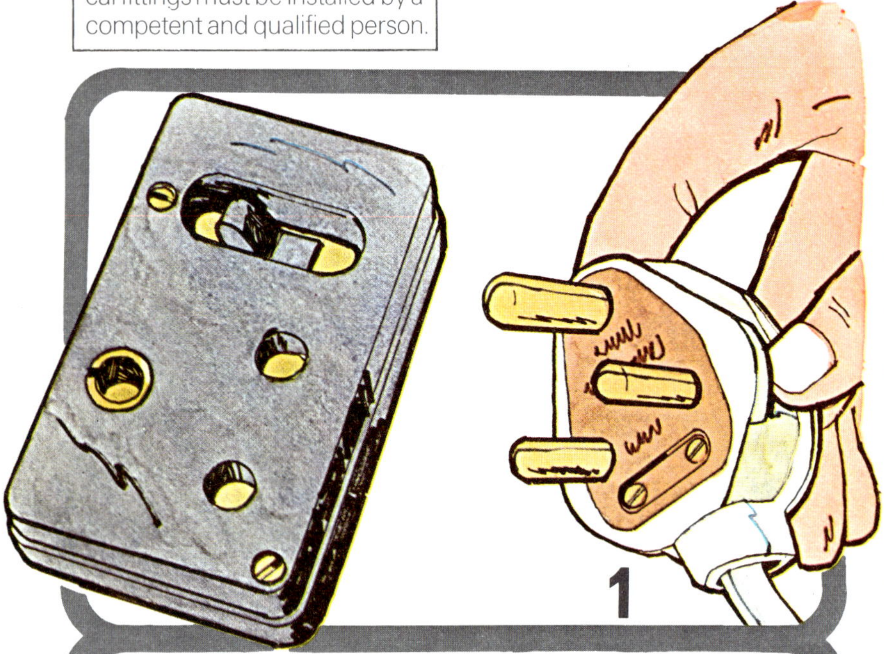

The wiring system of a house is connected into the underground or overhead Electricity Authority main, **A**. The connection from the main runs to a sealed Electricity Authority fuse unit inside the house, **B**.

The supply is run from the fuse unit to a sealed meter **C** where the consumption of the house is automatically registered. The wiring system of the house terminates adjacent to the meter in the form of household fused switch connections **D** and here the main supply is coupled up.

Electricity is a potentially dangerous force and fuses, which can be likened to a weak link in a chain, are necessary to protect the system in the event of a breakdown or overload. Fuses located at point **D** protect the house circuits and the type of housing unit depends basically on the age of the wiring system.

Older Systems

With older wiring systems (pre-1948) a separate fuse box and switch was installed for each circuit in the house. **Fig. 1** illustrates a typical non-fused round pin plug and socket as used with this type of radial wiring system. **Fig. 2** illustrates a typical metal clad fuse box. Three sizes of plug and socket were generally incorporated to

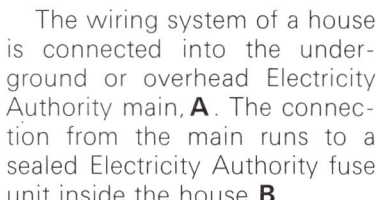

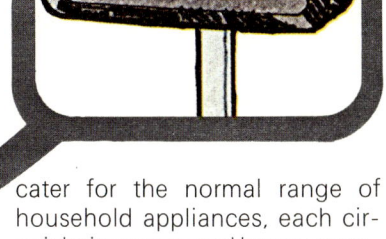

cater for the normal range of household appliances, each circuit being protected by an appropriate fuse located in a fuse box.

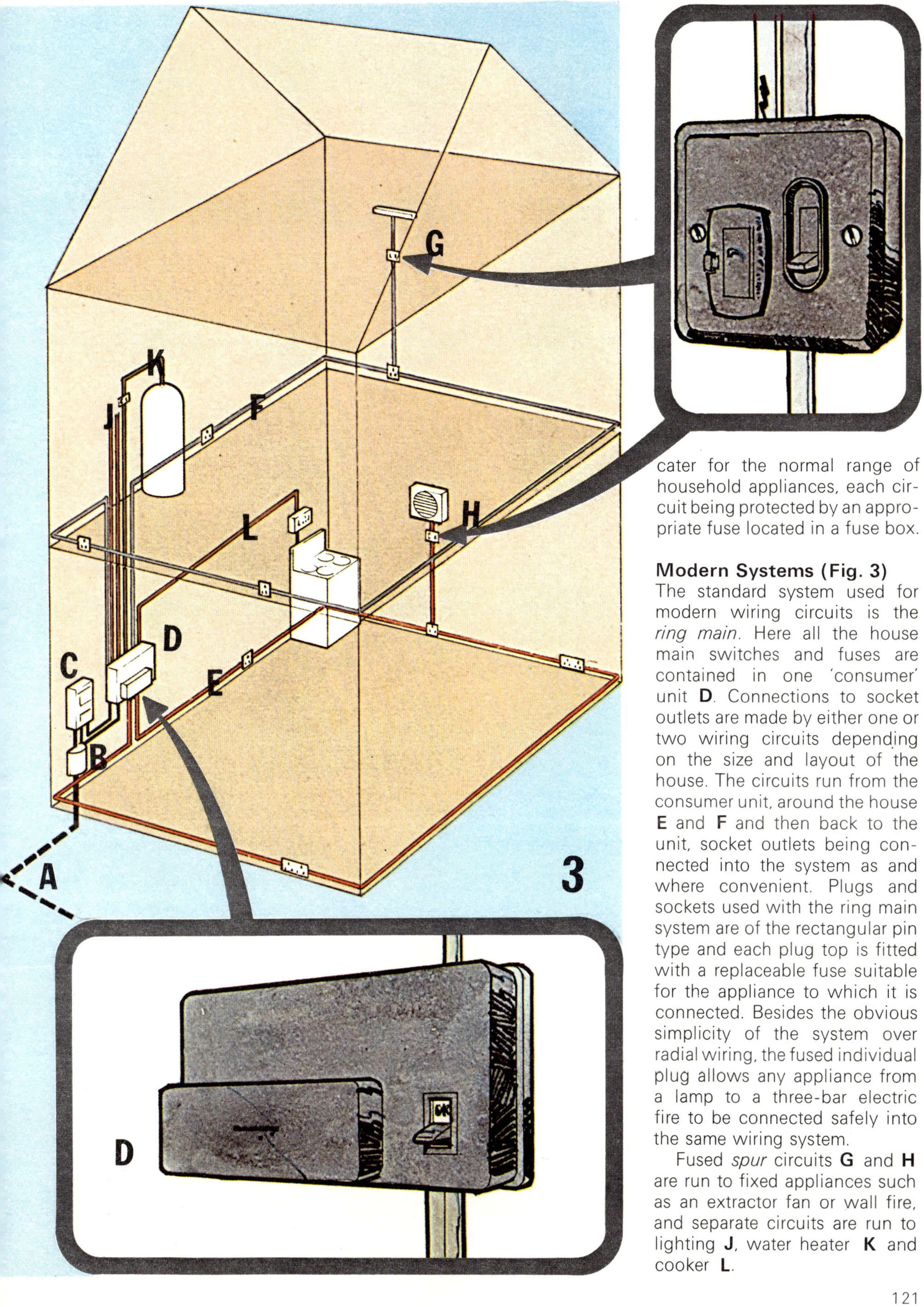

Modern Systems (Fig. 3)
The standard system used for modern wiring circuits is the *ring main*. Here all the house main switches and fuses are contained in one 'consumer' unit **D**. Connections to socket outlets are made by either one or two wiring circuits depending on the size and layout of the house. The circuits run from the consumer unit, around the house **E** and **F** and then back to the unit, socket outlets being connected into the system as and where convenient. Plugs and sockets used with the ring main system are of the rectangular pin type and each plug top is fitted with a replaceable fuse suitable for the appliance to which it is connected. Besides the obvious simplicity of the system over radial wiring, the fused individual plug allows any appliance from a lamp to a three-bar electric fire to be connected safely into the same wiring system.

Fused *spur* circuits **G** and **H** are run to fixed appliances such as an extractor fan or wall fire, and separate circuits are run to lighting **J**, water heater **K** and cooker **L**.

3

121

Tools and Materials

In order to tackle simple electrical jobs around the house, some basic tools are required which ideally should be kept together in a box. Fuses have a habit of blowing at inconvenient times, often after dark, and having the tools readily to hand helps to cope with the problem.

A. Torch, preferably of the free standing type, in order to leave both hands free.

B. Range of fuses to suit the household electrical system.

C. Two or three sizes of electrical screw drivers.

D. Pair of general purpose pliers.

E. Pair of purpose made wire strippers, for accurately stripping insulation from wire ends.

F. Pair of side cutters, for cutting heavy flex and cable.

G. Knife, for cutting through the outer sheathing of flex and cable.

Flexes and Cables

Multi-cored flexible wire is used for appliance leads, whilst the more rigid cable, generally with single metal cores, is used for fixed wiring. Both are available in a range of sizes and one capable of carrying an electrical load adequate for the appliance or circuit must be used. The cores of the flex or cable are coloured for identification and with modern flexes *Live* is **BROWN**, *Neutral* is **BLUE**, and *Earth* is **YELLOW/GREEN**. With cable and older flexes the colours are *Live* – **RED**, *neutral* – **BLACK**, *Earth* – **GREEN** (or bare wire).

All outlet sockets connected to the ring main system have three electrical connections. The *Live* and *Neutral* form an elec-

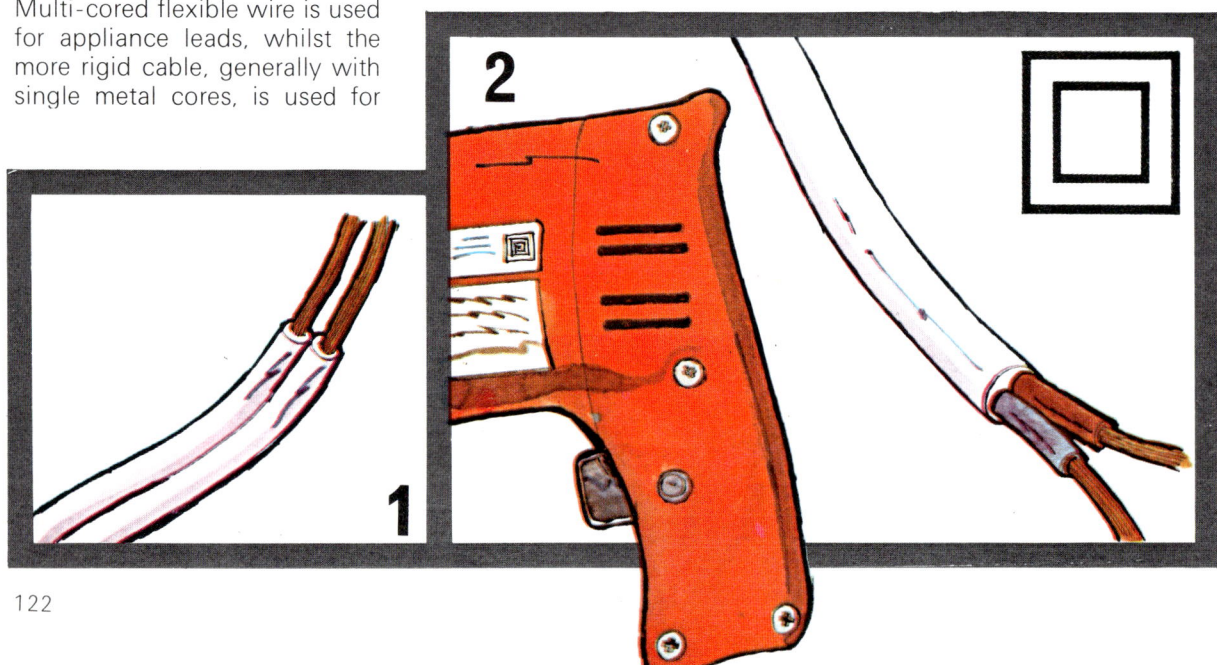

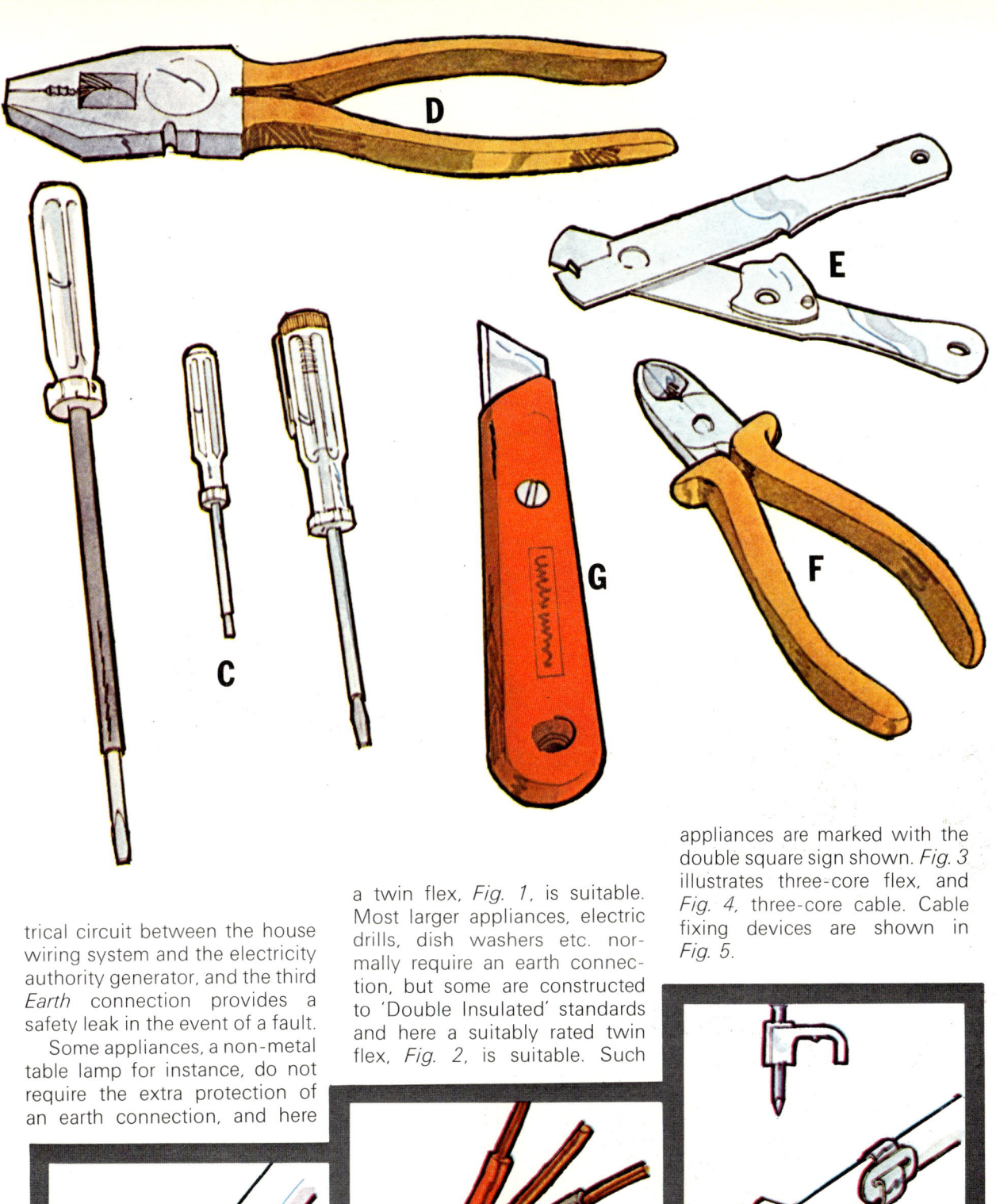

trical circuit between the house wiring system and the electricity authority generator, and the third *Earth* connection provides a safety leak in the event of a fault.

Some appliances, a non-metal table lamp for instance, do not require the extra protection of an earth connection, and here a twin flex, *Fig. 1*, is suitable. Most larger appliances, electric drills, dish washers etc. normally require an earth connection, but some are constructed to 'Double Insulated' standards and here a suitably rated twin flex, *Fig. 2*, is suitable. Such appliances are marked with the double square sign shown. *Fig. 3* illustrates three-core flex, and *Fig. 4*, three-core cable. Cable fixing devices are shown in *Fig. 5*.

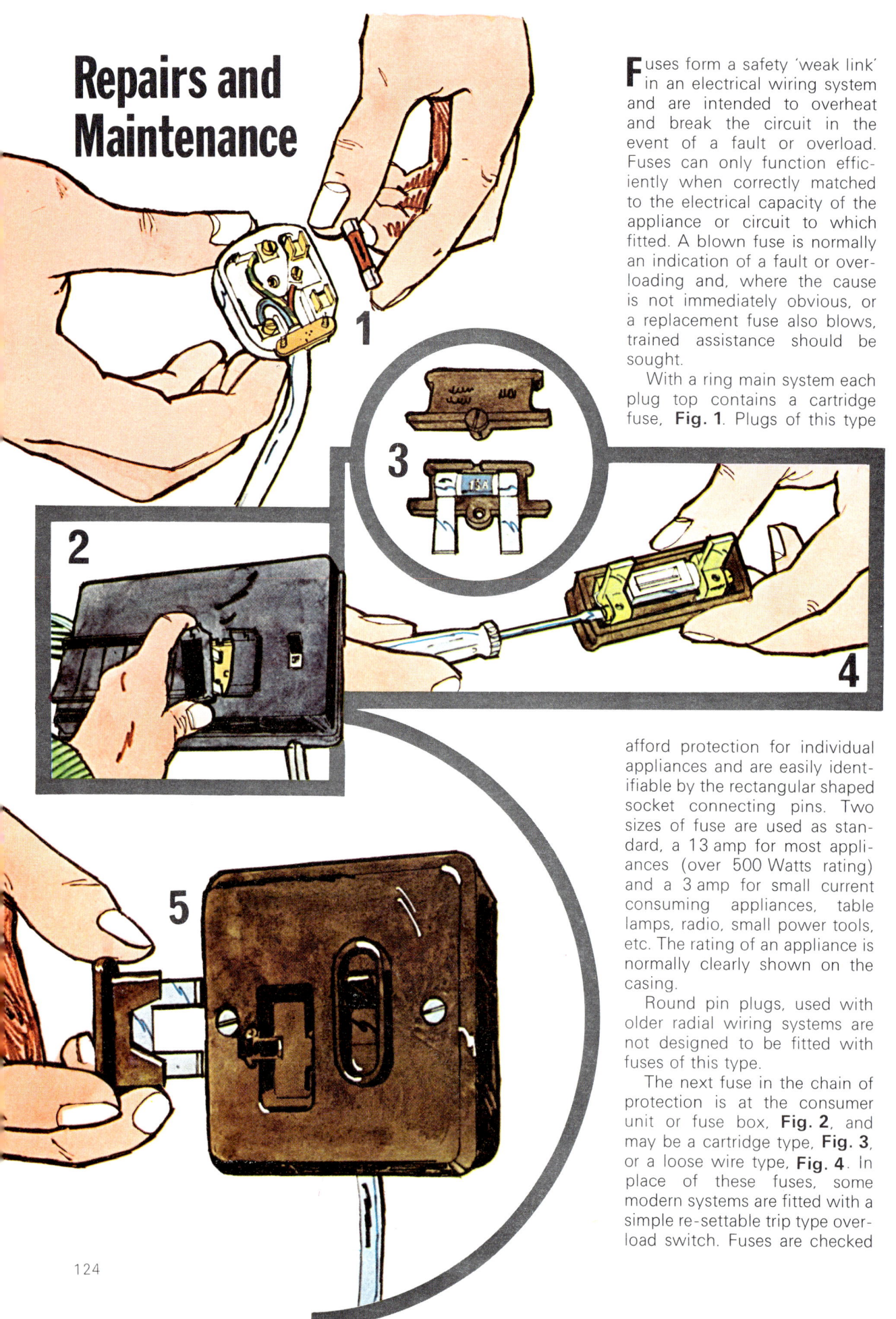

Repairs and Maintenance

Fuses form a safety 'weak link' in an electrical wiring system and are intended to overheat and break the circuit in the event of a fault or overload. Fuses can only function efficiently when correctly matched to the electrical capacity of the appliance or circuit to which fitted. A blown fuse is normally an indication of a fault or overloading and, where the cause is not immediately obvious, or a replacement fuse also blows, trained assistance should be sought.

With a ring main system each plug top contains a cartridge fuse, **Fig. 1**. Plugs of this type afford protection for individual appliances and are easily identifiable by the rectangular shaped socket connecting pins. Two sizes of fuse are used as standard, a 13 amp for most appliances (over 500 Watts rating) and a 3 amp for small current consuming appliances, table lamps, radio, small power tools, etc. The rating of an appliance is normally clearly shown on the casing.

Round pin plugs, used with older radial wiring systems are not designed to be fitted with fuses of this type.

The next fuse in the chain of protection is at the consumer unit or fuse box, **Fig. 2**, and may be a cartridge type, **Fig. 3**, or a loose wire type, **Fig. 4**. In place of these fuses, some modern systems are fitted with a simple re-settable trip type overload switch. Fuses are checked

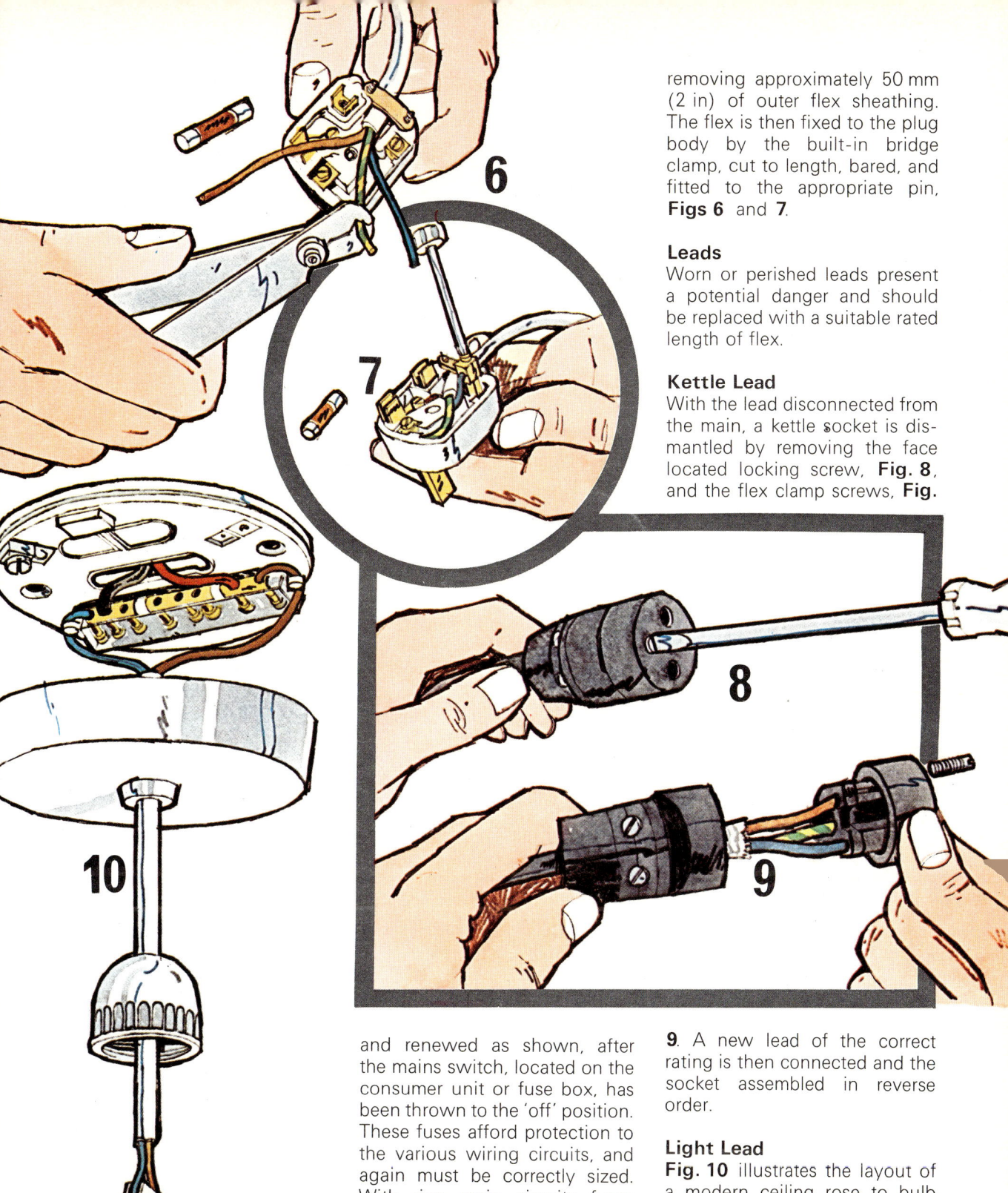

removing approximately 50 mm (2 in) of outer flex sheathing. The flex is then fixed to the plug body by the built-in bridge clamp, cut to length, bared, and fitted to the appropriate pin, **Figs 6** and **7**.

Leads
Worn or perished leads present a potential danger and should be replaced with a suitable rated length of flex.

Kettle Lead
With the lead disconnected from the main, a kettle socket is dismantled by removing the face located locking screw, **Fig. 8**, and the flex clamp screws, **Fig.**

and renewed as shown, after the mains switch, located on the consumer unit or fuse box, has been thrown to the 'off' position. These fuses afford protection to the various wiring circuits, and again must be correctly sized. With ring main circuits fuses are: lighting 5 amp, ring circuits 30 amp.

Individual protection is included for fixed appliances in a ring circuit by a fused spur, **Fig. 5**

Plugs and Leads
A plug top is fitted by firstly

9. A new lead of the correct rating is then connected and the socket assembled in reverse order.

Light Lead
Fig. 10 illustrates the layout of a modern ceiling rose to bulb holder wiring layout. With older metal clad fittings a third earthing connection may be included.

With the electricity supply turned off at the main switch, the fittings are dismantled as shown, **Fig. 10**, and a new length of flex fitted.

Acknowledgements

*The author would like to thank the following
for their help in preparing this book:*
  Robert Glover Studio: cover picture.
  Parry's (Retail) Ltd., Amersham, Bucks.
  The Cement and Concrete Association
  whose publications 'Concrete round the
  house' and 'Concrete in garden making'
  are available from Publications Sales Unit,
  Cement and Concrete Association,
  Wexham Springs, Slough SL3 6PL.

The Sure and Simple Series consists of 5 unique guides to Home Improvements, Gardening, Cooking and Crafts.

The amateur thinking of tackling an unfamiliar job in the house or garden will find these books invaluable.
Each one has been written by an expert who knows how to avoid the common pitfalls and is able to give explanations in clear, non-technical language. Each page has been carefully designed, and every step is illustrated with diagrams and easy to follow text.
The homemaker with neither much time nor much money will also find that this series is full of helpful hints which enable him to achieve professional results quickly, easily and cheaply.

SURE AND SIMPLE HOME MAKING by Jill Blake
Includes hints on planning, flooring, lighting, curtains and blinds, upholstery, coping with colour, schemes that work and finishing touches which give a home that extra special 'something'.

SURE AND SIMPLE COOKING by Alison Burt
A complete basic cookbook including a varied collection of interesting recipes for puddings and cakes, sauces, pasta and rice, meat and poultry, soups, fish dishes and herbs and spices.

SURE AND SIMPLE DO-IT-YOURSELF by Harry Butler
All aspects of maintaining and improving your home are covered including woodworking, decorating, plumbing, electricity, insulating, bricklaying, concreting and masonry, repairs and maintenance.

SURE AND SIMPLE GARDENING by Geoffrey Smith
A comprehensive gardening book covering vegetable gardening, lawn care, roses, pests and diseases, propagation, rock and water gardens, trees and shrubs and indoor plants.

HOMECRAFTS by Eve Harlow
An absorbing introduction to ten popular crafts: decoupage, corn dollies, stained glass, patchwork and quilting, pressed and dried flowers, block printing, batik, natural dyeing, Ikebana and pottery.